AS Music Listening Tests

Edexcel

Hugh Benham

and

Alistair Wightman

RHINEGOLD EDUCATION

www.rhinegoldeducation.co.uk

Music Study Guides

GCSE, AS and A2 Music Study Guides (AQA, Edexcel and OCR)
GCSE, AS and A2 Music Listening Tests (AQA, Edexcel and OCR)
AS/A2 Music Technology Study Guide (Edexcel)
AS/A2 Music Technology Listening Tests (Edexcel)
Revision Guides for GCSE (AQA, Edexcel and OCR), AS and A2 Music (Edexcel)

Other Rhinegold Study Guides

Rhinegold publishes resources for candidates studying Drama and Theatre Studies

Also available from Rhinegold Education

Key Stage 3 Listening Tests: Book 1 and Book 2
AS and A2 Music Harmony Workbooks
GCSE and AS Music Composition Workbooks
GCSE and AS Music Literacy Workbooks
Romanticism in Focus, Baroque Music in Focus, Modernism in Focus,
The Immaculate Collection in Focus, *Who's Next* in Focus,
Batman in Focus, *Goldfinger* in Focus, Musicals in Focus
Music Technology from Scratch
Dictionary of Music in Sound

First published 2010 in Great Britain by
Rhinegold Education
14–15 Berners Street
London W1T 3LJ
www.rhinegoldeducation.co.uk

© 2010 Rhinegold Education,
a division of Music Sales Limited

You should always check the current requirements of the examination, since these may change.
Copies of the Edexcel specification can be downloaded from the Edexcel website at www.edexcel.com.
Telephone: 01623 467467, Fax: 01623 450481, Email: publication.orders@edexcel.com

Edexcel AS Music Listening Tests
British Library Cataloguing in Publication Data.
A catalogue record for this book is available from the British Library.
Order No. RHG349
ISBN: 978-1-907447-10-5

Exclusive Distributors:
Music Sales Limited
Distribution Centre, Newmarket Road,
Bury St Edmunds, Suffolk, IP33 3YB, UK

Printed in the EU

Contents

The authors

Hugh Benham read Music and English at Southampton University, where he was awarded a PhD for his study of the music of John Taverner. He is a chair of examiners for GCE Music, an in-service trainer, church organist and writer, and formerly taught music in a sixth-form college. Hugh has contributed to *Music Teacher* and *Classroom Music* magazines, and is the author of *Baroque Music in Focus* (Rhinegold, 2nd ed. 2010). His other writing includes two books on English church music, including *John Taverner: his Life and Music* (Ashgate, 2003), articles on early music, contributions to *The New Grove Dictionary of Music and Musicians* (2001) and *Die Musik in Geschichte und Gegenwart*, and a complete edition of Taverner for *Early English Church Music*.

Alistair Wightman read Music at Oxford and then York University, where he was awarded a D. Phil for his study of the music of Karol Szymanowski. He has worked in primary, secondary and further education, and is a freelance teacher and writer as well as principal examiner in history and analysis for A-level music. His publications include *Writing about Music* (Rhinegold, 2008) and several books and articles devoted to Tadeusz Baird, Karłowicz and Szymanowski, including *Karłowicz, Young Poland and the Musical Fin-de-siècle* (Ashgate, 1996), *Karol Szymanowski: his Life and Music* (Ashgate, 1999) and *Szymanowski on Music: Selected Writings of Karol Szymanowski* (Toccata Press, 1999).

Acknowledgements

The authors would like to thank the consultant Paul Terry and the Rhinegold Education editorial and design team of Harriet Power and Ben Smith for their expert support in the preparation of this book.

General introduction

What this book is for

This book is to help you do as well as you possibly can in the Edexcel AS Music Unit 3 exam in 2011, 2012 or 2013, by providing you with test exercises, sample question papers and answers.

The contents of this book

This book begins with tests for Section A (Listening) of the Unit 3 exam. When working on Section A, make sure that you choose tests appropriate for the year you are sitting the exam, as there are different selections of set works in 2011, 2012 and 2013.

The insert contains one complete sample question paper for each year, covering Sections A, B (Investigating Musical Styles) and C (Understanding Chords and Lines). Do the test appointed for the year of your exam, because both Sections A and B are based on the particular selection of set works for that year. Section C, however, isn't related to the set works, and so, when you have completed the paper for your year, you will find it useful to work the Section C questions from the other papers for additional practice.

Mark schemes and answers are given at the back of the book, starting on page 67.

When working on Unit 3 you are not limited to the tests in this book. See the section 'How to find and invent more questions for Unit 3' on pages 64–66.

Recordings

For copyright reasons, this book has no CD with recordings of the music excerpts you will need to hear when you answer the Section A tests.

Recordings are available instead on the CDs that accompany the Edexcel *New Anthology of Music**. Each Section A test tells you which of the Edexcel CDs to use, which track, and what part of that track.

* Except for The Beatles' *A Day in the Life*: for this the recommended recording is Parlophone/EMI 0946 3 82419 2 8.

You are free to use recordings other than those from the Edexcel CDs, but you should be aware that you may encounter difficulties, not just with timings but with discrepancies arising from details of performance, such as tempi, balance and the like.

How to use this book

As previously noted, for Section A you must use tests that match your AS exam year – 2011, 2012 or 2013. Use them as practice in coping with the stresses and strains of the exam situation, but also work them in a more relaxed way to improve your knowledge, skills and understanding. It is perfectly all right to work some or all of the tests a second time when you have forgotten the answers.

When the exam is near, keep to the *five* playings of each Section A listening test that you will get in the exam. But earlier on, feel free to listen over and over until you get things right. Similarly, with Section C, take as long as you like in the early stages, but later on, consider how long you will be able to spend on each type of question in the exam.

How to do as well as you possibly can in the exam

1. **Read each question** – all of it – thoroughly and do exactly what it asks. You will have time to look at the questions before the exam begins. Because the music will be from set works that you should know well, you will probably be able to spot one or two answers before the music is played – but always check any such predicted answers carefully when you do hear the music.

2. **Don't panic.** Prepare thoroughly, and this should give you the confidence to do your best.

3. **Concentrate.** There is no time to let your attention wander, especially in Section A, where there can be ten or more parts to each question, and five chances to hear the music.

4. **Manage your time carefully.** In particular, don't get bogged down with questions whose answers you really don't know or can't remember.

5. **Make sufficient points** to gain the number of marks available. Take note of the bracketed sub-totals after questions. For example, '(3)' means 'three marks': to get all these you will need to make three valid points. Let's imagine that two marks are available for a question whose answer you decide is 'a sequence'. That alone (if correct) will get one mark. Consider what else might be needed to gain the second mark – for example, is it a *rising* sequence or a *falling* sequence?

6. **Lots of words don't always earn lots of marks.** Be as concise as reasonably possible, and always **relevant**. If a question is about texture and you write about tonality, you won't get any marks, however true your comments might be – you will just have wasted valuable time. But it is only common sense to use a whole phrase or sentence to explain a point if you can't think of the right technical words in the heat of the moment. Nevertheless…

7. **Whenever you can, use the accepted technical words** (imitation, sequence and the like). Remember also: the questions themselves often use such technical words – so if you don't understand them, you won't be able to answer correctly.

> If you come across technical words that you don't understand when working the tests in this book, consult a dictionary such as the Rhinegold *Dictionary of Music in Sound* by David Bowman.

Introduction to Section A (Listening)

The Unit 3 exam begins with listening questions based on two of the set works you have studied from the Edexcel Anthology of Music.

> The set works for the years 2011–2013 are listed in the specification, pages 59–61.

Questions and part-questions

Question 1 in your exam will be based on an excerpt from one of the set works in the **Instrumental Music** area of study. Question 2 will be based on an excerpt from a set work in the **Vocal Music** area of study.

You won't know which works will feature in these questions until you open your exam paper, so you must study every work with equal care.

Each Listening question will have a number of parts, labelled alphabetically. You must answer all of them. One or more parts will be multiple choice, and for these you have to answer by putting a cross in a box. Some other parts will require one- or two-word answers, phrases or sentences. After each part you'll see in brackets how many marks it is worth: where two or more marks are available, you are expected to make the same number of valid points.

In Section A answers you can use continuous prose where appropriate, but it's not necessary. You will not be marked on quality of written communication, as in Section B answers, but you should still aim to get spellings right (especially words frequently mis-spelt such as 'bass' and 'rhythm').

Most parts of a listening question will relate to just a few bars (starting at or near the beginning and then working through the passage). There may also be one or more general parts. These may require some knowledge of the whole piece from which the excerpt is taken – you must know, for instance, what the form is, and you may have to recognise what part of the piece the excerpt comes from.

In this book we have mainly chosen excerpts that do not come from the beginning of a piece. This is to remind you that examiners are free to do this, and to help you get used to the fact that in such cases the numbering of bars in the skeleton score will always start at 1, wherever the passage comes from in a set work.

The majority of tests appear for the first time in this volume, but where set works for 2011–2013 are repeats of those prescribed for 2009 and 2010, we have reused tests from the previous edition of *AS Music Listening Tests*.

Listening to the excerpts

In the exam, the music for each question will be played to you five times on a CD. There will be timed pauses between playings and after the final playing, to allow you to write your answers. The lengths of the pauses will be announced.

When you work tests from this book, you must supply your own recordings, as explained above (page 5). You will have to time the pauses yourself, or ask someone else to help you, in accordance with the instructions on page 9.

Skeleton scores in the exam

You won't have a complete copy of the Anthology in the exam, but a separate booklet will contain 'skeleton scores' of the two excerpts you will hear. Each skeleton score will provide you with outline musical notation, on a single stave (or possibly on two staves, according to Edexcel's online tutor support materials). The skeleton score will probably have the principal melodic line at least some of the time. Elsewhere it may show the bass line, or may just provide the rhythm. Exactly what you're given will depend on what you're asked about: it's very unlikely that the pitches of the melodic line for bars 5–8 will be printed if you have to recognise a melodic sequence in these bars, for example.

Each skeleton score will have bar numbers. If an excerpt is taken from the start of a set work, the bar numbers of the skeleton score will be the same as those of the Anthology. Where an excerpt comes from later in a work, the bar numbers of the skeleton score will be numbered from 1 onwards (as we said above), so they won't in this case match the numbering of the Anthology. When you answer about details of melody, chords and texture, this is no problem: you're hardly likely to have learned each set work literally bar-by-bar. It does mean, however, that if you're asked about where an excerpt comes within the whole piece, you will need to rely on the *sound* of the music, not just on remembering (for example) that this must be the development section because it's labelled bar 80.

Skeleton scores will have 'cues' to help you. For example, if you are asked to identify the key and cadence at a particular point, the words 'Key and cadence?' are likely to appear on the skeleton score in the appropriate bar(s).

During the exam, remember to:

1. **Read the questions** during the time allowed for this before the music is played for the first time. If you think you already know any answers, jot them down at this point: confirm (or change) them later.

2. **Read each part of each question thoroughly.** Do exactly what it tells you.

3. **Note how many marks are awarded for each part.** Don't get bogged down with a hard one-mark question. With questions worth two or more marks, try to make enough points to qualify for all the marks available.

4. **Keep calm.** It's possible to get flustered when you first see a question, with all its various parts. But remember:

   ➢ There are always at least one or two quite easy bits
   ➢ Some, if not many or most, of the answers may come to you during or after the third, fourth and fifth playings. Don't panic if, early on, your paper has a lot of blank spaces.

Section A (Listening)

When working the listening tests that follow, you will need a copy of the CDs that accompany the Edexcel Anthology of Music. For each test, you are told which CD to use, which track, and which part of that track. In the early stages, you can listen to each excerpt as many times as you like, and need not time the pauses between listenings. But when practising for the exam, give yourself a minute or two to read the questions, and then follow the procedure shown below (or ask someone else to operate the CD player and time the pauses):

➢ Play the music for the first time, followed by a 30-second pause
➢ Play the music for the second time, followed by a one-minute pause
➢ Play the music for the third time, followed by a one-minute pause
➢ Play the music for the fourth time, followed by a 30-second pause
➢ Play the music for the fifth and final time, followed by a three-minute pause, during which you should finish your answers.

Tests for 2011

You will find eight tests below based on the set works for 2011. Tests on Instrumental Music and Vocal Music are presented as one mixed group rather than as two separate groups, to encourage you to practise both areas of study equally. There are two other Section A tests for 2011 in the sample examination paper on pages 1–10 of the insert.

On finding and inventing additional Section A questions, see pages 64–66.

2011 Test 1   **CD 4 Track 15, 3:06–4:04**

You will hear an excerpt from *Don't look back in anger* by Noel Gallagher. A skeleton score of this excerpt is provided below. Bar numbers in this question refer to the skeleton score.

(a)   Bars 1, 3 and 5 all begin with an F major chord.

    (i)   How does the harmony change on the **third crotchet beat** of each of these bars?*

    .... **(1)**

> * You can describe the change (e.g. in terms of major and minor), or give a chord symbol.

    (ii)   What chord is used in bars 2, 4 and 6?

    .... **(1)**

(b)   Name the scale used by the lead guitar in bars 5 to 6.

    .... **(1)**

(c)   Comment on the lead guitar part in bar 7.

....

.... (3)

(d)   What happens in bar 12?

....

.... (2)

(e)   Complete the chord chart below:

Bar 13, beats 1–2: ....C...........

Bar 13, beats 3–4: ....

Bar 14, beats 1–2: ....

Bar 14, beats 3–4: ....   (3)

(f)   Contrast the vocal part of bar 16 (beat 4) to 17 (beat 4) with the vocal part of bar 13.

....

....

.... (3)

(g)   Put a cross in the box next to the statement that is true.*

☒ **A** The excerpt features a turnaround

☒ **B** The excerpt features a middle eight

☒ **C** The excerpt features an instrumental and chorus

☒ **D** The excerpt features the introduction and verse   (1)

> * This question relies on your study of the whole song, whereas most questions deal with a few bars from the skeleton score and test your listening skills (although even here previous knowledge of the music often helps).

(h)   Name the style of this song.

....   (1)

(Total 16 marks)

2011 Test 2   **CD 3 Track 8, 1:05–2:53**

You will hear an excerpt from *Locus iste* by Bruckner. A skeleton score of this excerpt is provided below. Bar numbers in this question refer to the skeleton score.

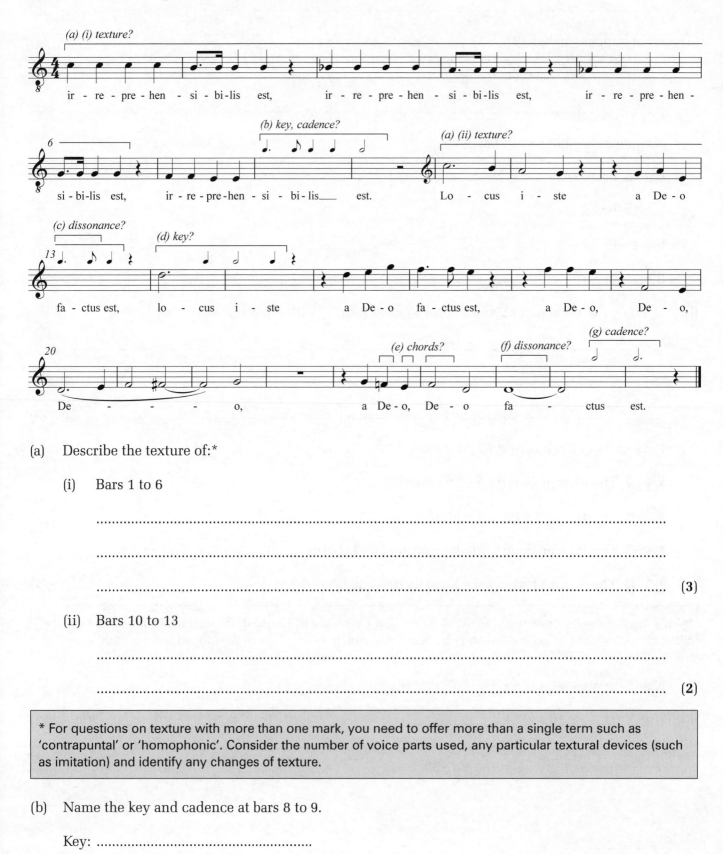

(a)   Describe the texture of:*

(i)   Bars 1 to 6

....

....

.... **(3)**

(ii)   Bars 10 to 13

....

.... **(2)**

> * For questions on texture with more than one mark, you need to offer more than a single term such as 'contrapuntal' or 'homophonic'. Consider the number of voice parts used, any particular textural devices (such as imitation) and identify any changes of texture.

(b)   Name the key and cadence at bars 8 to 9.

Key: ....

Cadence: ....   **(2)**

(c)   Name the type of dissonance used at bar 13 (beats 1–2).

.... **(1)**

(d)   Name the key at bars 14 to 15.

.... **(1)**

(e)   Complete the following table of chords:

Bar 24, beat 2: ....Ib...........

Bar 24, beat 3: ....

Bar 24, beat 4: ....

Bar 25, beats 1 to 2: .... **(3)**

(f)   Name the type of dissonance heard throughout bar 26.

.... **(1)**

(g)   What type of cadence is heard at bars 27 to 28?

.... **(1)**

(h)   Put a cross in the box next to the statement that is true.

☒ **A** This excerpt is taken from an anthem

☒ **B** This excerpt is taken from a hymn

☒ **C** This excerpt is taken from a madrigal

☒ **D** This excerpt is taken from a motet **(1)**

(i)   Put a cross in the box next to the statement that is true.

☒ **A** The excerpt was composed in the Baroque period

☒ **B** The excerpt was composed in the Classical period

☒ **C** The excerpt was composed in the Renaissance period

☒ **D** The excerpt was composed in the Romantic period **(1)**

(Total 16 marks)

2011 Test 3   **CD 2 Track 5, 1:50–3:11**

You will hear an excerpt from the fourth movement of String Quartet in E♭, Op. 33 No. 2 ('The Joke') by Haydn. A skeleton score of this excerpt is provided below. Bar numbers in this question refer to the skeleton score.

(a) Name the cadence at bars 7 to 8.*

....

(1)

> * Don't guess, but remember that in music of this style most cadences are perfect or imperfect. Interrupted cadences have an element of surprise. Plagal cadences are uncommon.

(b) Precisely describe the harmonic device used in bars 8 to 12.

.... (2)

(c) Describe the texture of bars 12 (last quaver beat) to 16.

....

....

.... (3)

(d) Describe the melodic device used in bars 25 to 26.

.... (2)

(e) Describe the harmony at bars 40 to 41.

....

....

.... (3)

(f) How do the chords at the beginnings of bars 51 and 53 differ from one another?

....

.... (2)

(g) How many bars' rest are there in the given part after bar 67?

....

(1)

(h) Put a cross in the box next to the statement that is true.

The overall structure of the piece from which this excerpt is taken is:

☒ **A** Binary   ☒ **B** Rondo   ☒ **C** Sonata form   ☒ **D** Ternary   (1)

(i) Put a cross in the box next to the statement that is true.

☒ **A** The excerpt comes from a Baroque work

☒ **B** The excerpt comes from a Classical work

☒ **C** The excerpt comes from an early Romantic work

☒ **D** The excerpt comes from a late Romantic work   (1)

(Total 16 marks)

2011 Test 4   **CD 1 Track 6, 2:24–3:37**

You will hear an excerpt from the first movement of Concerto for Double String Orchestra by Tippett. A skeleton score of this excerpt is provided below. Bar numbers in this question refer to the skeleton score.

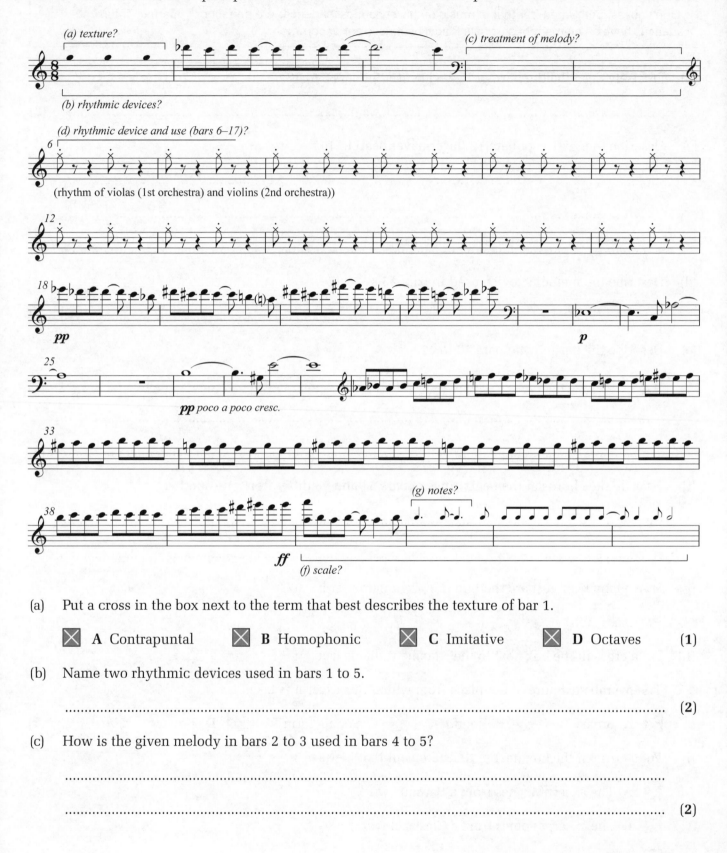

(a)   Put a cross in the box next to the term that best describes the texture of bar 1.

    ☒ **A** Contrapuntal   ☒ **B** Homophonic   ☒ **C** Imitative   ☒ **D** Octaves   **(1)**

(b)   Name two rhythmic devices used in bars 1 to 5.

.... **(2)**

(c)   How is the given melody in bars 2 to 3 used in bars 4 to 5?

....

.... **(2)**

(d) (i) Name the rhythmic device used in bars 6 to 17 to develop the first four notes from bar 2.*

....

(1)

* Listen to the lower parts: don't be distracted by the printed rhythmic ostinato.

(ii) Explain in detail how it is used.

....

....

....

(3)

(e) Describe the texture in bars 40 to 43.

....

....

(2)

(f) What type of scale is used in the highest sounding (violin 1) part in bars 40 to 43?

....

(1)

(g) Give the letter names of the first two notes printed above the stave in bar 41.

....

(2)

(h) Put a cross in the box next to the term that best describes the style of this music.

☒ **A** Classical   ☒ **B** Neoclassical   ☒ **C** Romantic   ☒ **D** Serial   (1)

(i) Put a cross in the box next to the statement that is true.

☒ **A** The excerpt is a bridge passage

☒ **B** The excerpt is the opening of the second subject

☒ **C** The excerpt is the end of the development and start of the recapitulation

☒ **D** The excerpt is the coda

(1)

(Total 16 marks)

2011 Test 5   **CD 4 Track 13, 1:48–2:40**

You will hear an excerpt from *You can get it if you really want* by Jimmy Cliff (recorded by Desmond Dekker and the Aces). A skeleton score of this excerpt is provided below. Bar numbers in this question refer to the skeleton score.

(a)   How are the reeds, brass and bass used in bars 2 to 9?

....

.... **(2)**

(b)   Describe the rhythmic patterns used in the guitar and drum parts in bars 3 to 5.

....

.... **(2)**

(c)   Describe the harmony in bars 6 to 9.

....

....

.... **(3)**

(d)   Complete the following table of chords:*

Bar 14: ....Dβ............

Bar 15: ....

Bar 16: ....

Bar 17: ....   **(3)**

> * In questions on popular music and jazz, chords are best described using chord symbols (E♭, Gm, etc.), as the table above makes clear. Notice how the given chord for bar 14 'sets the scene' and help you hear bars 15–17 in context.

(e)   Comment on the writing for lead and backing vocals in bars 20 to 23.

....

....

.... **(3)**

(f)   Give a single word to describe the texture of this excerpt.

.... **(1)**

(g)   Put a cross in the box next to the statement that is most accurate.

⊠ **A** The lead vocal line in this excerpt draws on the major scale

⊠ **B** The lead vocal line in this excerpt draws on the minor scale

⊠ **C** The lead vocal line in this excerpt draws on the pentatonic scale

⊠ **D** The lead vocal line in this excerpt draws on the whole-tone scale   **(1)**

(h)   Put a cross in the box next to the statement that is true.

⊠ **A** This excerpt starts with the end of a verse

⊠ **B** This excerpt starts with the introduction

⊠ **C** This excerpt starts with the end of the chorus

⊠ **D** This excerpt starts with a turnaround   **(1)**

(Total 16 marks)

2011 Test 6   **CD 3 Track 19, 1:15–2:24**

You will hear an excerpt from 'Summertime' from *Porgy and Bess* by George Gershwin, DuBose and Dorothy Heyward and Ira Gershwin. A skeleton score of this excerpt is provided below. Bar numbers in this question refer to the skeleton score.

(a)   Describe the writing for backing vocals in bars 2 to 4.

....

.... **(2)**

(b)   Describe the accompaniment in bars 2 to 4.

....

.... **(2)**

(c)   Name the rhythmic device used in the given part in bar 6.

.... **(1)**

(d)   Name the harmonic device used at bar 8, third crotchet beat.

.... **(1)**

(e)   Name the type of scale used in the vocal part of bars 14 and 15.

.... **(1)**

(f)   Explain how the printed part in bars 16 to 20 is changed in this performance.

....

.... (2)

(g)   Name the type of scale used in the highest part of the backing vocals in bars 17 to 20.

.... (1)

(h)   Name the cadence used at bars 19 to 20.

.... (1)

(i)   Describe the orchestral writing from bar 20 to the end of the excerpt.

....

....

.... (3)

(j)   Put a cross in the box next to the statement that is true.

The overall structure of the song from which this excerpt is taken is:

☒ **A** Binary   ☒ **B** Strophic   ☒ **C** Through-composed   ☒ **D** Twelve-bar blues   (1)

(k)   Put a cross in the box next to the statement that is true.

The date of the first performance of this piece was:

☒ **A** 1916   ☒ **B** 1936   ☒ **C** 1956   ☒ **D** 1976   (1)

(Total 16 marks)

2011 Test 7   **CD 1 Track 15, 1:49–2:30**

You will hear an excerpt from the first movement of *Sequenza III* by Berio. A skeleton score of this excerpt is provided below. The numbers above the staves (in rectangular boxes) are timings in minutes and seconds, calculated from the beginning of the excerpt.

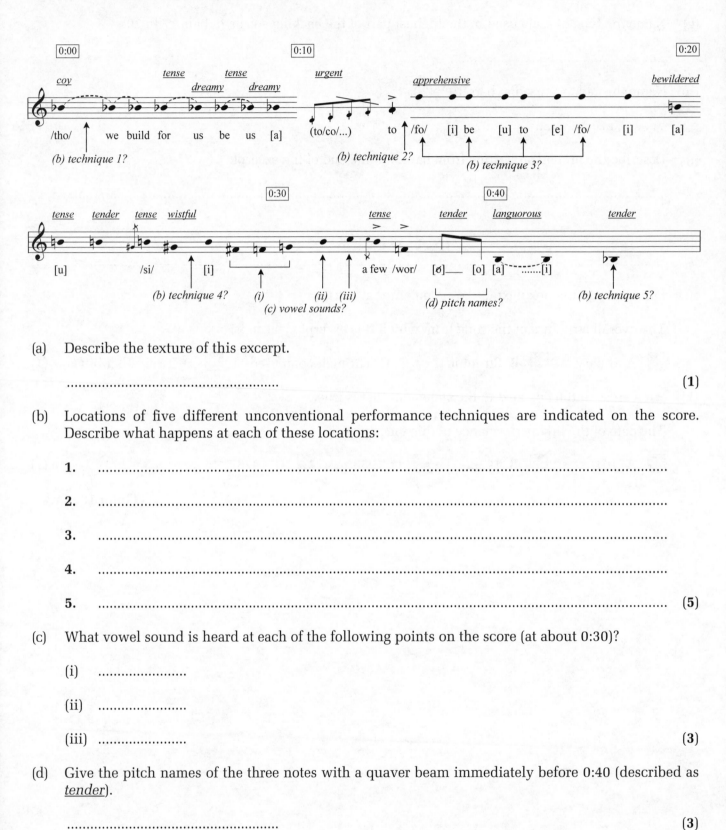

(a)   Describe the texture of this excerpt.

....   **(1)**

(b)   Locations of five different unconventional performance techniques are indicated on the score. Describe what happens at each of these locations:

   1.   ....

   2.   ....

   3.   ....

   4.   ....

   5.   ....   **(5)**

(c)   What vowel sound is heard at each of the following points on the score (at about 0:30)?

   (i)   ....

   (ii)   ....

   (iii)   ....   **(3)**

(d)   Give the pitch names of the three notes with a quaver beam immediately before 0:40 (described as *tender*).

....   **(3)**

(e) Put a cross in the box next to the statement that is true.

The work from which this excerpt is taken is best described as:

☒ **A** Avant-garde   ☒ **B** Minimalist   ☒ **C** Post-modern   ☒ **D** Serial   **(1)**

(f) Put a cross in the box next to the statement that is true.

The work from which this excerpt is taken dates from:

☒ **A** 1950   ☒ **B** 1966   ☒ **C** 1982   ☒ **D** 1998   **(1)**

(g) In what respect does the anthology score as a whole give only approximate guidance to the performer?

....

.... **(2)**

(Total 16 marks)

2011 Test 8   **CD 1 Track 10, 1:59–3:10**

You will hear an excerpt from the first movement of Quartet Op. 22 by Webern. A skeleton score of this excerpt is provided below. Bar numbers in this question refer to the skeleton score.

(a)   Name the instrument that plays each of the motifs marked (i)–(iv) in bars 1 to 4:

    (i)   ....

    (ii)   ....

    (iii)   ....

    (iv)   ....   **(4)**

(b)   How does the writing in bars 7 to 8 differ from that in the preceding bars?

    ....

    ....   **(2)**

(c)   What performance direction (not shown in the skeleton score) is given to the violinist at each of the following notes?

   (i)   the E♭ in bar 11: ....

   (ii)   the D♮ in bar 11: ....   **(2)**

(d)   Describe the texture of bars 13 to 18 and the role of the various instruments in it.

   ....

   ....

   ....

   ....   **(4)**

(e)   Identify the melodic intervals:

   (iii) Between the first two notes in bar 17: ....

   (iv)   Between the last two notes of the excerpt: ....   **(2)**

(f)   Put a cross in the box next to the statement that is true.

   The overall structure of the piece from which this excerpt is taken is:

   ☒ **A** Binary   ☒ **B** Rondo   ☒ **C** Sonata form   ☒ **D** Theme and variations   **(1)**

(g)   Put a cross in the box next to the statement that is true.

   ☒ **A** This excerpt is taken from an expressionist work

   ☒ **B** This excerpt is taken from an impressionist work

   ☒ **C** This excerpt is taken from a minimalist work

   ☒ **D** This excerpt is taken from a serial work   **(1)**

(Total 16 marks)

Tests for 2012

You will find eight tests below based on the set works for 2012. Tests on Instrumental Music and Vocal Music are presented as one mixed group rather than as two separate groups, to encourage you to practise both areas of study equally. There are two other Section A tests for 2012 in the sample examination paper on pages 11–20 of the insert.

On finding and inventing additional Section A questions, see pages 64–66.

2012 Test 1   **CD 1 Track 3, 5:08–6:02**

You will hear an excerpt from the third movement of *Harold in Italy* by Berlioz. A skeleton score of this excerpt is provided below. Bar numbers in this question refer to the skeleton score.

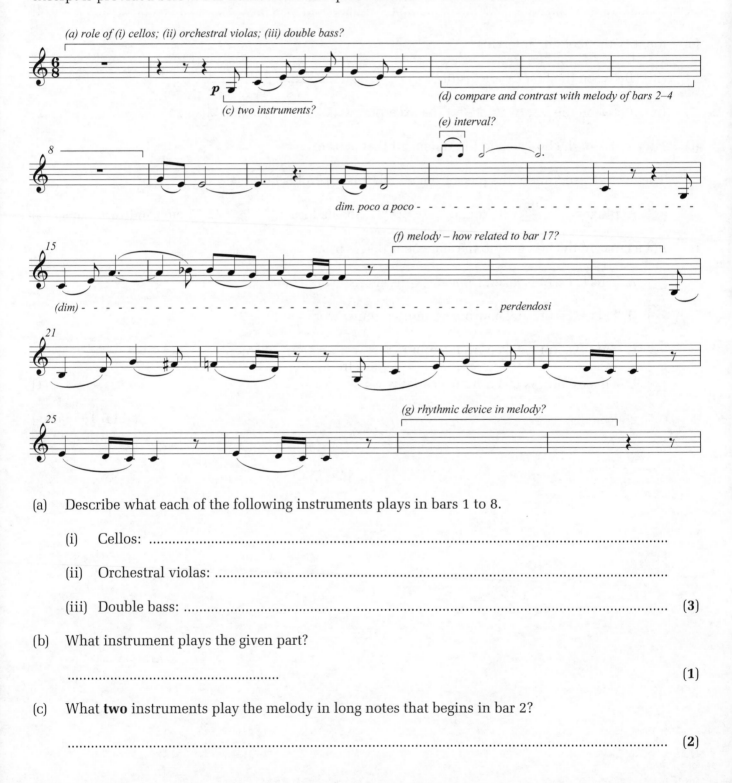

(a)   Describe what each of the following instruments plays in bars 1 to 8.

    (i)   Cellos: ....

    (ii)   Orchestral violas: ....

    (iii) Double bass: .... **(3)**

(b)   What instrument plays the given part?

    .... **(1)**

(c)   What **two** instruments play the melody in long notes that begins in bar 2?

    .... **(2)**

(d) Compare and contrast the printed melody in bars 2 to 4 with the melody played by the same instrument in bars 5 to 7.

....

....

.... **(3)**

(e) Name the interval in the given part in bar 12.*

.... **(2)**

> * To gain the full mark in questions that require you to name an interval, you should normally give a two-word answer (such as major 2nd or diminished 5th), except in the case of a perfect octave, where the single word 'octave' is sufficient. This remains true whether the question is worth one mark or two marks.

(f) How is the melody in bars 18 to 20 related to the melody of bar 17?

....

.... **(2)**

(g) Name the rhythmic device used in the melody of bars 27 to 28.

.... **(1)**

(h) Put a cross in the box next to the statement that is true.

The work from which this excerpt is taken is a:

☒ **A** Concerto   ☒ **B** Sonata   ☒ **C** Symphony   ☒ **D** Symphonic poem   **(1)**

(i) Put a cross in the box next to the statement that is true.

The work from which this excerpt is taken dates from:

☒ **A** 1734   ☒ **B** 1784   ☒ **C** 1834   ☒ **D** 1884   **(1)**

(Total 16 marks)

2012 Test 2   **CD 3 Track 15, 1:53–3:31**

You will hear an excerpt from *My mother bids me bind my hair* by Haydn. A skeleton score of this excerpt is provided below. Bar numbers in this question refer to the skeleton score.

(a)   Describe the texture of bars 1 to 2.

    .... **(1)**

(b)   Name the dissonance at the word 'stone' in bar 6.

    .... **(1)**

(c)   Name the cadence and the key at the words 'none can hear' (bars 7 to 8).*

    Cadence: ....

    Key: ....   **(2)**

* Don't guess, but remember that in music of this style most cadences are perfect or imperfect. If a piece begins in a major key, most major-key cadences tend to be in the tonic key or in the dominant – which is it here?

(d) What type of scale is used in the vocal part from bars 14 (6th quaver) to 16 (1st quaver)?

.... **(1)**

(e) Describe the piano accompaniment in bars 14 to 18.

....

....

.... **(3)**

(f) What key is heard in passing at bar 21?

.... **(1)**

(g) Complete the following chord chart:

Bar 22, quaver 1: ....Ib.............

Bar 22, quaver 3: ....

Bar 22, quaver 4: ....

Bar 22, quaver 6: .... **(3)**

(h) Comment on the piano part of bar 27.

....

.... **(2)**

(i) Put a cross in the box next to the statement that is true.

The overall structure of the piece from which this excerpt is taken is:

☒ **A** Binary   ☒ **B** Strophic   ☒ **C** Through-composed   ☒ **D** Verse and chorus   **(1)**

(j) Suggest a date of composition for this song.

.... **(1)**

(Total 16 marks)

2012 Test 3   **CD 2 Track 4, 1:29–2:06**

You will hear an excerpt from the fourth movement of Trio Sonata in D, Op. 3 No. 2 by Corelli. A skeleton score of this excerpt is provided below. Bar numbers in this question refer to the skeleton score.

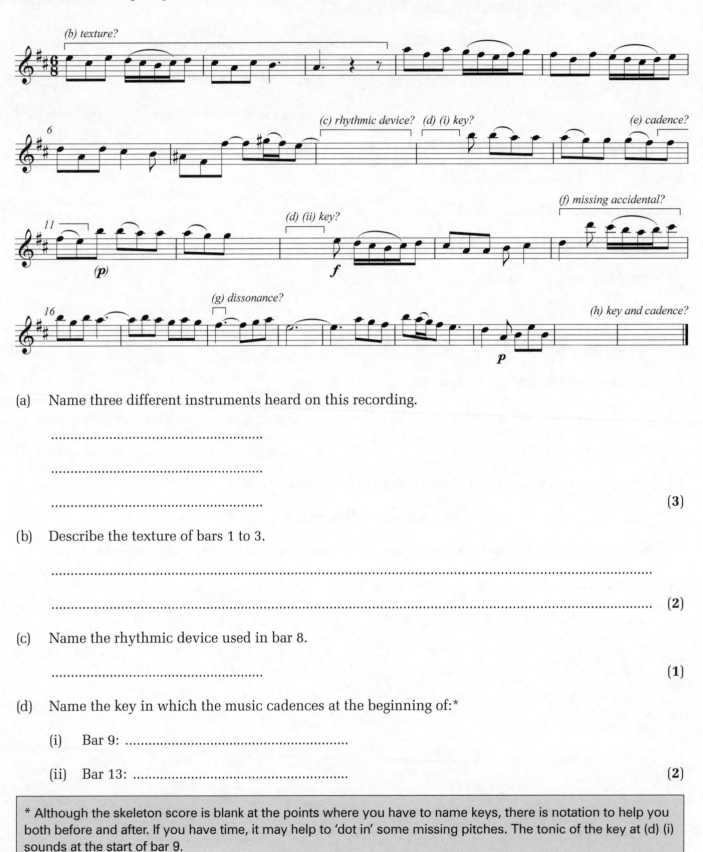

(a)   Name three different instruments heard on this recording.

   ....

   ....

   ....   **(3)**

(b)   Describe the texture of bars 1 to 3.

   ....

   ....   **(2)**

(c)   Name the rhythmic device used in bar 8.

   ....   **(1)**

(d)   Name the key in which the music cadences at the beginning of:*

   (i)   Bar 9: ....

   (ii)   Bar 13: ....   **(2)**

> * Although the skeleton score is blank at the points where you have to name keys, there is notation to help you both before and after. If you have time, it may help to 'dot in' some missing pitches. The tonic of the key at (d) (i) sounds at the start of bar 9.

(e)   What type of cadence is used in bars 10 to 11?

   ....   **(1)**

(f)   Name the accidental missing from bar 15 of the skeleton score.

      ....   **(1)**

(g)   Name the type of dissonance heard at the beginning of at bar 18.

      ....   **(1)**

(h)   Give the key and cadence at the end of the excerpt.

      Key: ....

      Cadence: ....   **(2)**

(i)   From what type of multi-movement work does this excerpt come?

      ....   **(1)**

(j)   Put a cross in the box next to the statement that is true.

      The movement from which this excerpt is taken is:

      ☒ **A** In binary form   ☒ **B** A fugue   ☒ **C** A rondo   ☒ **D** In sonata form   **(1)**

(k)   Put a cross in the box next to the statement that is true.

      The work from which this excerpt is taken was first published in:

      ☒ **A** 1649   ☒ **B** 1689   ☒ **C** 1729   ☒ **D** 1769   **(1)**

                                                              (Total 16 marks)

2012 Test 4 CD 3 Track 9, 0:32–2:09

You will hear an excerpt from the third movement of *Symphony of Psalms* by Stravinsky. A skeleton score of this excerpt is provided below. Bar numbers in this question refer to the skeleton score.

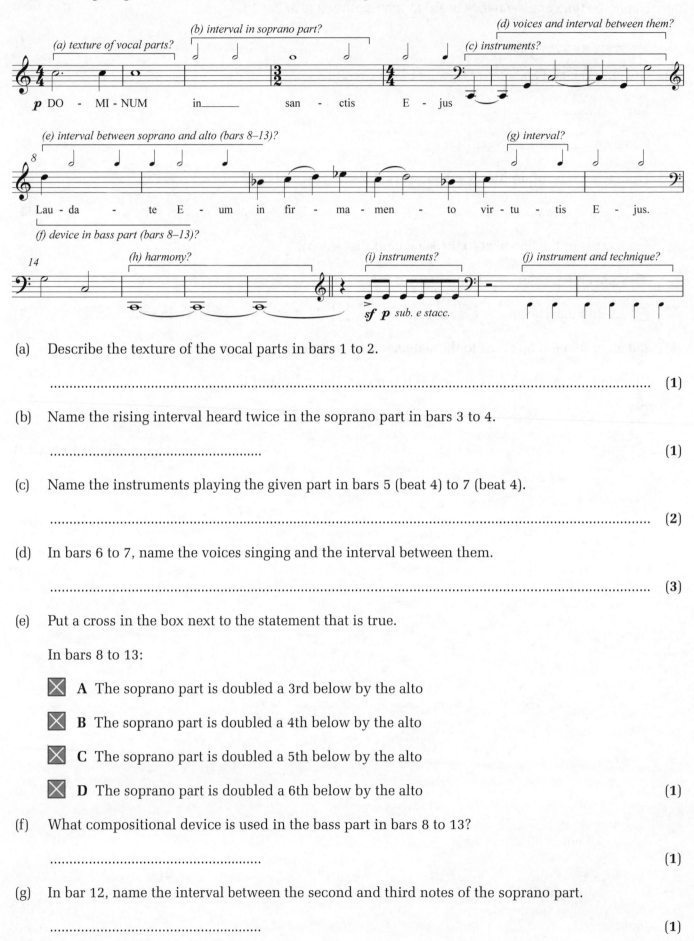

(a) Describe the texture of the vocal parts in bars 1 to 2.

.... **(1)**

(b) Name the rising interval heard twice in the soprano part in bars 3 to 4.

.... **(1)**

(c) Name the instruments playing the given part in bars 5 (beat 4) to 7 (beat 4).

.... **(2)**

(d) In bars 6 to 7, name the voices singing and the interval between them.

.... **(3)**

(e) Put a cross in the box next to the statement that is true.

In bars 8 to 13:

☒ **A** The soprano part is doubled a 3rd below by the alto

☒ **B** The soprano part is doubled a 4th below by the alto

☒ **C** The soprano part is doubled a 5th below by the alto

☒ **D** The soprano part is doubled a 6th below by the alto **(1)**

(f) What compositional device is used in the bass part in bars 8 to 13?

.... **(1)**

(g) In bar 12, name the interval between the second and third notes of the soprano part.

.... **(1)**

(h) Describe the harmony in bars 15 to 17.*

....

.... (2)

---

* Questions on harmony may require you to identify chords in terms of Roman numerals (I, IV, Vb, etc.) or chord symbols (Gm, F⁷, etc.), or may be more open (as here). More 'open' harmony questions may expect, for example, references to *types* of chords, or to chord progressions, or to special harmonic features (such as a false relation or tierce de Picardie).

(i) What instruments play the quaver motif in bar 18?

.... (2)

(j) Name the instrument playing the bass part of bars 19 to 20, and give the term for the playing technique used here.

.... (2)

(Total 16 marks)

2012 Test 5   **CD 2 Track 6, 6:00–7:16**

You will hear an excerpt from the first movement of Septet in E♭, Op. 20 by Beethoven. A skeleton score of this excerpt is provided below. Bar numbers in this question refer to the skeleton score.

(a)   Put a cross in the box next to the term that best describes the texture at the beginning (up to the end of bar 4):

    ⊠ **A** Counterpoint   ⊠ **B** Homophony   ⊠ **C** Mainly octaves   ⊠ **D** Unison   **(1)**

(b)   Name the instruments playing the given part at:

    (i)   Bars 5 to 9: ....

    (ii)   Bars 9 to 13: ....

    (iii)   Bars 14 to 17: ....   **(3)**

(c) Name the key at:

  (i) Bars 16 to 17 (quaver 1): ....

  (ii) Bars 20 to 21: .... **(2)**

(d) Describe the woodwind parts in bars 24 to 29.*

....

.... **(2)**

> * It is not necessary to name the two instruments involved. Your answer might refer to any two of the following points: articulation (do the woodwind play legato or staccato, for example?); rhythm; the interval between the woodwind instruments.

(e) Name the harmonic device used in bars 29 to 42.

.... **(2)**

(f) Describe the chord outlined in the bass in bars 40 to 42.

.... **(1)**

(g) What type of scale is used in bars 49 to 50?

.... **(1)**

(h) Name the ornament in bar 52.

.... **(1)**

(i) Name the cadence in bars 52 to 53.

.... **(1)**

(j) Put a cross in the box next to the statement that is true.

  ☒ **A** The excerpt is the opening of the exposition

  ☒ **B** The excerpt is the development and start of the recapitulation

  ☒ **C** The excerpt is the end of the recapitulation and start of the coda

  ☒ **D** The excerpt is a bridge passage **(1)**

(k) Put a cross in the box next to the statement that is true.

  The work from which this excerpt comes was first performed in:

  ☒ **A** 1740   ☒ **B** 1770   ☒ **C** 1800   ☒ **D** 1830 **(1)**

(Total 16 marks)

2012 Test 6

The music is not available on the *NAM* recordings for copyright reasons. The recommended recording is Parlophone/EMI 0946 3 82419 2 8.

You will hear an excerpt from *A Day in the Life* by The Beatles. A skeleton score of this excerpt is provided below. Bar numbers in this question refer to the skeleton score.

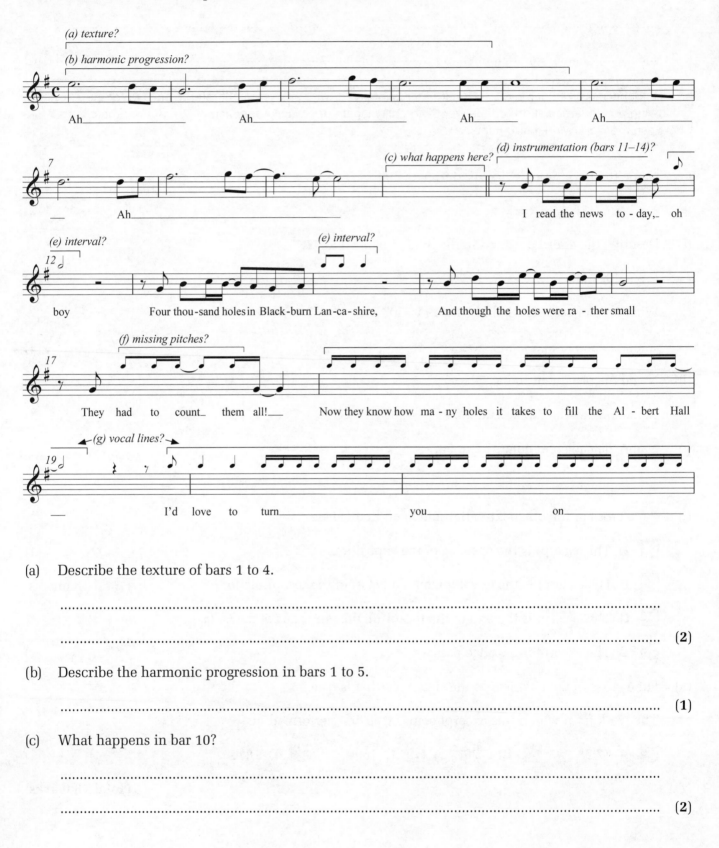

(a)   Describe the texture of bars 1 to 4.

   ....

   .... **(2)**

(b)   Describe the harmonic progression in bars 1 to 5.

   .... **(1)**

(c)   What happens in bar 10?

   ....

   .... **(2)**

(d)   How does the instrumentation of bars 11 to 14 differ from that of bars 1 to 4?

....

.... **(2)**

(e)   Contrast the interval in the vocal part on 'oh boy' (bars 11 to 12) with the interval on 'Lancashire' (bar 14).

....

.... **(2)**

(f)   Supply the missing pitches in bar 17:

They had   to   count_   them all!___   **(3)**

(g)   Compare and contrast the vocal lines of bars 18 to 19 (second crotchet beat) with 19 (last quaver) to 21.

....

....

.... **(3)**

(h)   Put a cross in the box next to the statement that is true.

☒ **A** The excerpt contains an atonal link

☒ **B** The excerpt is the end of the verse and start of a transition

☒ **C** The excerpt is a transition and final verse

☒ **D** The excerpt is the final verse and outro   **(1)**

(Total 16 marks)

2012 Test 7   **CD 3 Track 12, 0:23–1:06**

You will hear an excerpt from *Sing we at pleasure* by Weelkes. A skeleton score of this excerpt is provided below. Bars numbers in this question refer to the skeleton score.

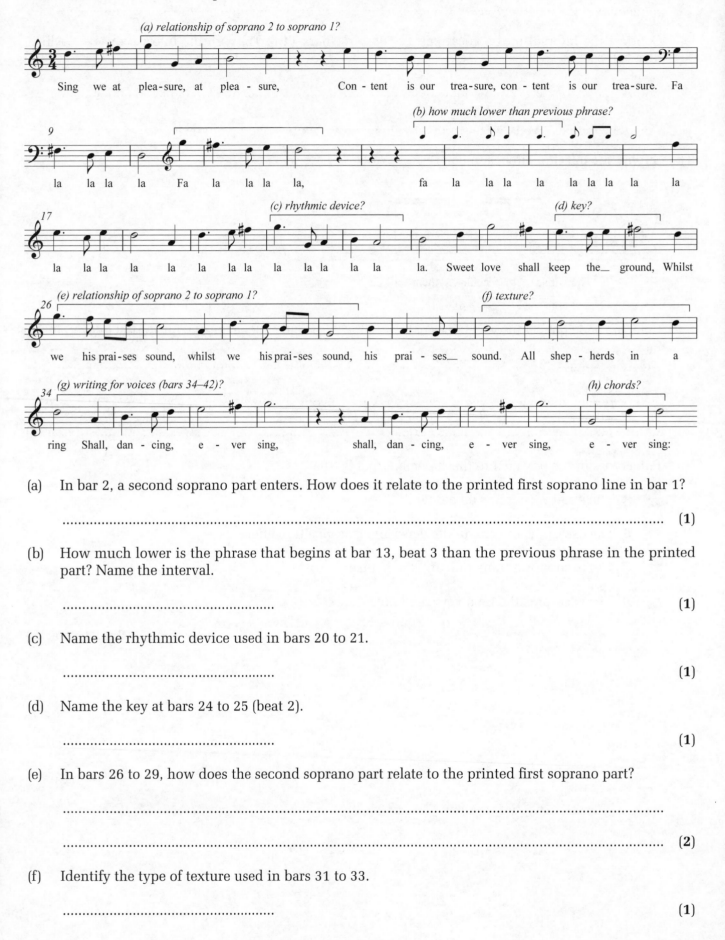

(a)   In bar 2, a second soprano part enters. How does it relate to the printed first soprano line in bar 1?

....   **(1)**

(b)   How much lower is the phrase that begins at bar 13, beat 3 than the previous phrase in the printed part? Name the interval.

....   **(1)**

(c)   Name the rhythmic device used in bars 20 to 21.

....   **(1)**

(d)   Name the key at bars 24 to 25 (beat 2).

....   **(1)**

(e)   In bars 26 to 29, how does the second soprano part relate to the printed first soprano part?

....

....   **(2)**

(f)   Identify the type of texture used in bars 31 to 33.

....   **(1)**

(g) Comment on the writing for voices in bars 34 to 42.

....

....

....

.... **(4)**

(h) Complete the following table of chords:

Bar 41, beat 3: ....G major in first inversion...........

Bar 42, beat 1: ....

Bar 42, beat 3: ....

Bar 43, beat 1: .... **(3)**

(i) From what type of vocal piece is this excerpt taken?

.... **(1)**

(j) Put a cross in the box next to the term that best describes the structure of the music from which the excerpt is taken.

☒ **A** Binary   ☒ **B** Strophic   ☒ **C** Through-composed   ☒ **D** Tripartite   **(1)**

(Total 16 marks)

2012 Test 8   **CD 3 Track 9, 5:51–7:23**

You will hear an excerpt from the third movement of *Symphony of Psalms* by Stravinsky. A skeleton score of this excerpt is provided below. Bar numbers in this question refer to the skeleton score.

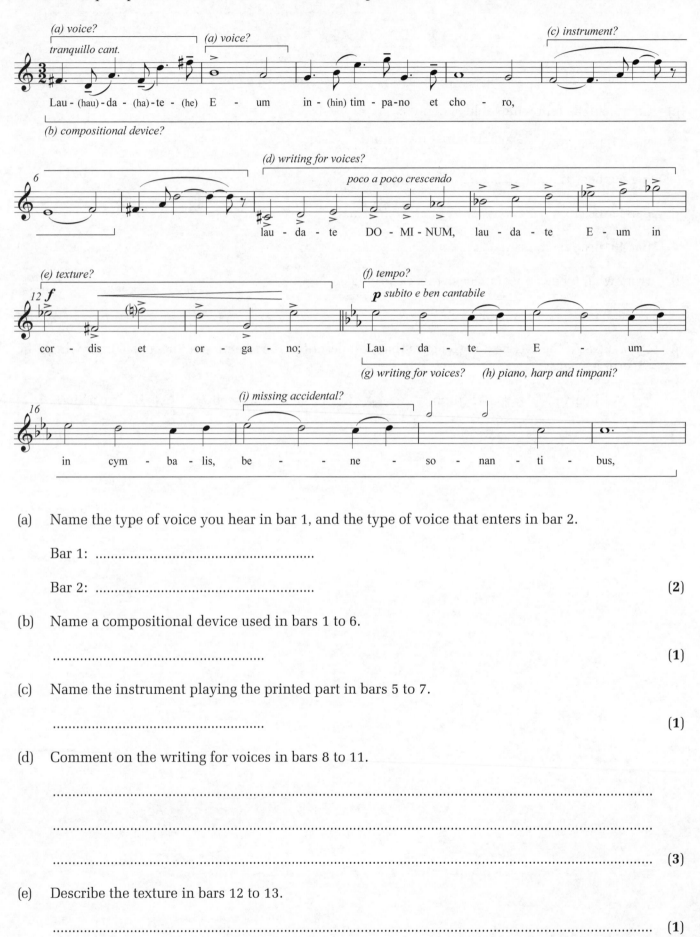

(a)   Name the type of voice you hear in bar 1, and the type of voice that enters in bar 2.

Bar 1: ....

Bar 2: ....   **(2)**

(b)   Name a compositional device used in bars 1 to 6.

....   **(1)**

(c)   Name the instrument playing the printed part in bars 5 to 7.

....   **(1)**

(d)   Comment on the writing for voices in bars 8 to 11.

....

....

....   **(3)**

(e)   Describe the texture in bars 12 to 13.

....   **(1)**

(f)   Is the passage starting in bar 14 faster, slower or at the same tempo as the preceding section?

....   **(1)**

(g)   Comment on the writing for voices in bars 14 to 19.

....

....

....   **(3)**

(h)   Comment on the rhythm and melody of the line played by piano, harp and timpani in bars 14 to 19.

....

....   **(3)**

(i)   An accidental has been omitted from bar 17. Insert it at the appropriate point on the stave below:

                                                                                                                                                                         (1)

(Total 16 marks)

Tests for 2013

You will find eleven tests below based on the set works for 2013. Tests on Instrumental Music and Vocal Music are presented as one mixed group rather than as two separate groups, to encourage you to practise both areas of study equally. There are two other Section A tests for 2013 in the sample examination paper on pages 21–30 of the insert.

On finding and inventing additional Section A questions, see pages 64–66

2013 Test 1   **CD 1 Track 5, 7:01–8:25**

You will hear an excerpt from *Prélude à l'après-midi d'un faune* by Debussy. A skeleton score of this excerpt is provided below. Bar numbers in this question refer to the skeleton score.

(a)   Name the instrument playing the given part at:

(i)   Bars 1 to 2: ....

(ii)   Bars 3 to 5 (first quaver): ....

(iii) Bars 5 (third crotchet beat) to 9 (first crotchet beat): ....   **(3)**

(b)   Describe the accompaniment in bars 5 to 6.

....

....

....   **(3)**

(c)   Comment on the melodic writing in bar 9.*

....

....

.... **(3)**

---

* Try to make three separate points in order to earn all three marks. The 'comment' here should go beyond simple description – the key to the question is to note how bar 9 relates to the preceding melodic passage.

(d)   How does bar 10 relate to bar 9?

.... **(1)**

(e)   Describe the woodwind writing in bar 11.

....

.... **(2)**

(f)   How do bars 12 to 15 relate to bars 5 to 8?

....

.... **(2)**

(g)   Put a cross in the box next to the statement that is true.

The excerpt is:

☒ **A** The end of the first part of the piece and beginning of the central episode

☒ **B** The end of the central section and start of a varied reprise of the main theme

☒ **C** The start of the coda

☒ **D** The section containing the final appearance of the main theme   **(1)**

(h)   Put a cross in the box next to the statement that is true.

The work from which this excerpt comes was first performed in:

☒ **A** 1854   ☒ **B** 1874   ☒ **C** 1894   ☒ **D** 1914   **(1)**

(Total 16 marks)

2013 Test 2   **CD 3 Track 3, 0:00–1:10**

You will hear an excerpt from *Ohimè, se tanto amate* by Monteverdi. A skeleton score of this excerpt is provided below. Bar numbers in this question refer to the skeleton score.

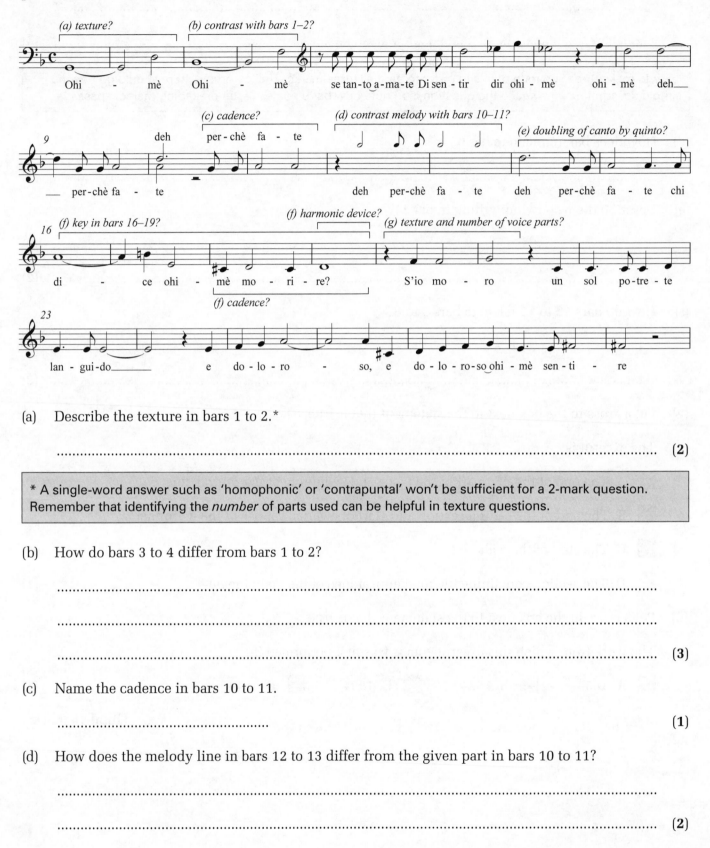

(a)   Describe the texture in bars 1 to 2.*

.... **(2)**

> * A single-word answer such as 'homophonic' or 'contrapuntal' won't be sufficient for a 2-mark question. Remember that identifying the *number* of parts used can be helpful in texture questions.

(b)   How do bars 3 to 4 differ from bars 1 to 2?

....

....

.... **(3)**

(c)   Name the cadence in bars 10 to 11.

.... **(1)**

(d)   How does the melody line in bars 12 to 13 differ from the given part in bars 10 to 11?

....

.... **(2)**

(e)   Put a cross in the box next to the statement that is true.

The given part (canto) in bars 14 to 15 is doubled by the other soprano part (quinto):

☒   **A** A third below

☒   **B** A third above

☒   **C** A sixth below

☒   **D** A sixth above   (1)

(f)   Complete the following statements:

The key of the music in bars 16 to 19 is .... The cadence in bars

18 to 19 is ...., and the harmonic device used on the last chord is

a ....   (3)

(g)   Name the type of texture in bars 20 to 21 (second crotchet beat), and identify the number of voice parts heard.

.... (2)

(h)   In what bar do you hear all five voices singing together for the **first** time?*

....   (1)

* When the full five-part choir sings, you should be conscious of greater weight, density and richness than elsewhere.

(i)   Put a cross in the box next to the statement that is true.

☒   **A** This excerpt is taken from an anthem

☒   **B** This excerpt is taken from a madrigal

☒   **C** This excerpt is taken from a cantata

☒   **D** This excerpt is taken from an opera   (1)

(Total 16 marks)

2013 Test 3   **CD 2 Track 8, 0:00–0:55**

You will hear an excerpt from the first movement of Sonata for Horn, Trumpet and Trombone by Poulenc. A skeleton score of this excerpt is provided below. Bar numbers in this question refer to the skeleton score.

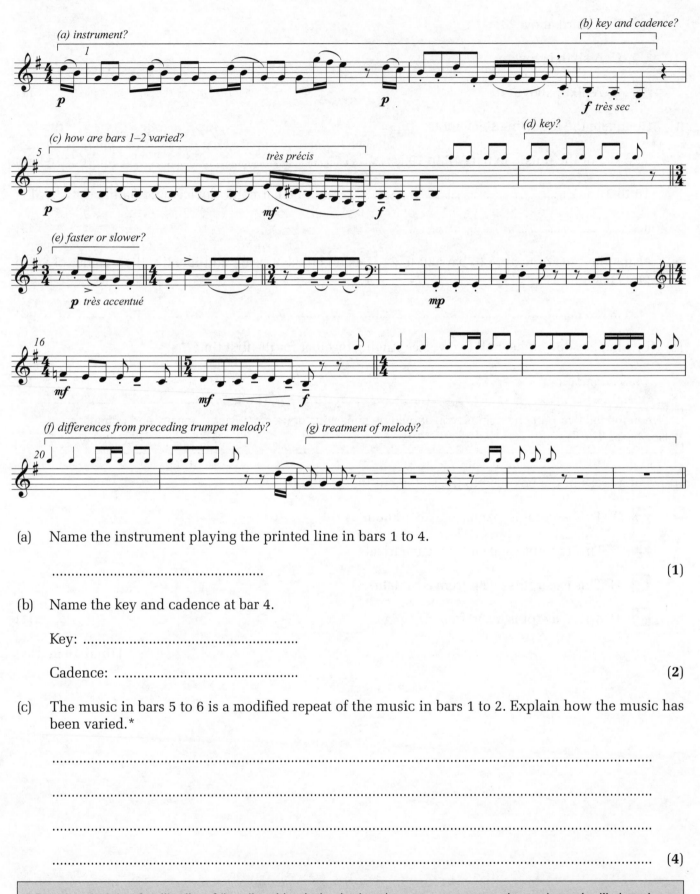

(a) Name the instrument playing the printed line in bars 1 to 4.

....   **(1)**

(b) Name the key and cadence at bar 4.

Key: ....

Cadence: ....   **(2)**

(c) The music in bars 5 to 6 is a modified repeat of the music in bars 1 to 2. Explain how the music has been varied.*

....

....

....

....   **(4)**

> * Bear in mind that familiar list of 'headings' (melody, rhythm, harmony, texture and so on): you're likely to have to address more than one of these to be able to find the four points necessary to score fully on this question.

(d)   Name the key at bar 8.

....   **(1)**

(e)   Is the music faster or slower at bar 9?

....   **(1)**

(f)   How does the trumpet melody in bars 20 to 21 differ from that in bars 18 to 19?

....

....

....   **(3)**

(g)   How does Poulenc treat the melody in bars 22 to 25?

....

....   **(2)**

(h)   Put a cross in the box next to the statement that is true.

☒   **A** The excerpt is part of a binary form movement

☒   **B** The excerpt is part of a sonata form movement

☒   **C** The excerpt is part of a rondo

☒   **D** The excerpt is the first part of a ternary form movement   **(1)**

(i)   Put a cross in the box next to the statement that is true.

☒   **A** This work is best described as Classical

☒   **B** This work is best described as modern

☒   **C** This work is best described as Neoclassical

☒   **D** This work is best described as Romantic   **(1)**

(Total 16 marks)

2013 Test 4   **CD 4 Track 10, 1:20–2:13**

You will hear an excerpt from *I'm Leavin' You* by Howlin' Wolf. A skeleton score of this excerpt is provided below. Bar numbers in this question refer to the skeleton score.

(a)   Describe the vocal style used in bars 3 and 5.

....   **(1)**

(b)   Name the instrument playing the printed part in bar 4.

....   **(1)**

(c)   Some 'blue-note' accidentals have been omitted from the given part of bar 6. Insert them at the appropriate places on the stave below.

                                                                                                                          (2)

(d)   Name the instrument playing the rhythm shown above the stave in bars 11 to 12.

....   **(1)**

Unit 3 test papers

This booklet contains three practice papers, one for each of the years 2011 to 2013.

Test paper for 2011

The test paper below has questions for all three sections of Unit 3. Answer all questions, but note that there is a choice in Question 3, where you can answer on the area of study Instrumental Music or on the area of study Vocal Music.

Allow yourself 5 minutes' reading time before starting work on the paper. The two hours allowed to complete the test paper must start after the 5 minutes have been used up.

The Section A questions (Questions 1 and 2) together should take between 25 and 30 minutes, including the timed pauses. If possible, someone other than yourself should operate the CD player and time the pauses – you will have enough to do with listening to the music and answering the questions! The timing of pauses is shown on page 9 of the main book.

Keep an eye on the clock as you work through Sections B and C. In Section B you must work from memory, and not use a copy of the anthology. You need not quote bar numbers, unless they easily come to mind – but try to give examples of at least some points, noting for example that a long dominant pedal occurs 'near the end'. For Question 5 only, you can check your work on a piano or keyboard (use headphones if other students are working the paper at the same time as you).

Section A: Listening

Answer both questions.

Question 1   **CD 2 Track 12, 2:45–3:44**

You will hear an excerpt from one of the movements you have studied from Partita No. 4 in D (BWV 828) by J.S. Bach. A skeleton score of this excerpt is provided below. Bar numbers in this question refer to the skeleton score.

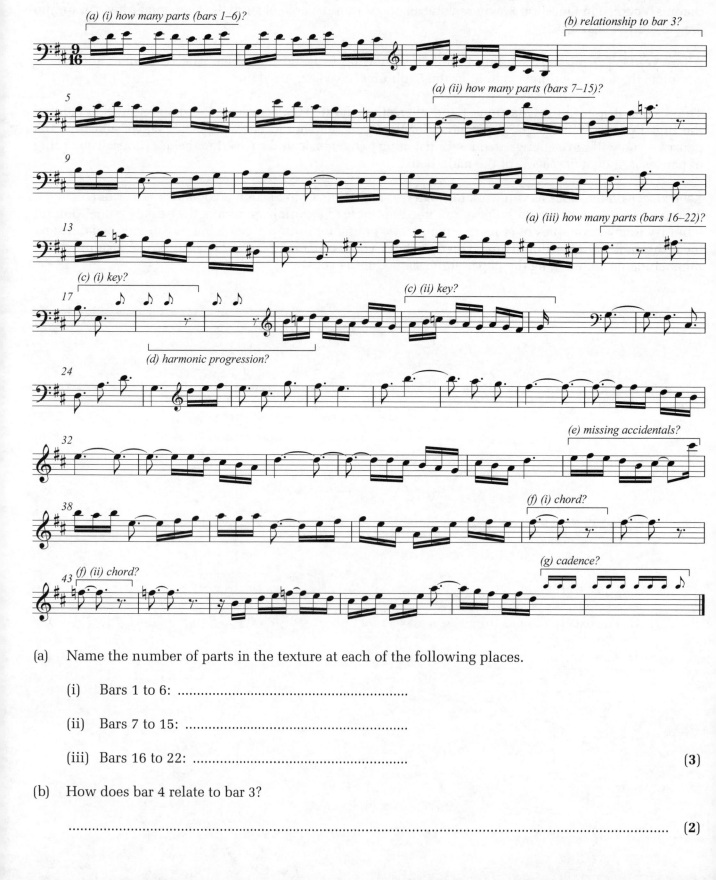

(a)   Name the number of parts in the texture at each of the following places.

    (i)   Bars 1 to 6: ....

    (ii)   Bars 7 to 15: ....

    (iii)   Bars 16 to 22: ....   **(3)**

(b)   How does bar 4 relate to bar 3?

.... **(2)**

(c) Name the keys at:

    (i) Bars 17 to 18: ....

    (ii) Bars 21 to 22 (beat 1): .... **(2)**

(d) Identify the harmonic progression at bars 18 to 20 (beat 1).

.... **(1)**

(e) In bar 37, add the two missing accidentals.

    (2)

(f) Describe the chords at:

    (i) Bar 41: ....

    (ii) Bar 43: .... **(2)**

(g) Name the cadence at the end of the excerpt.

.... **(1)**

(h) Put a cross in the box next to the statement that is true.

    The piece from which this excerpt is taken is:

    ☒ **A** In binary form   ☒ **B** A fugue   ☒ **C** In ritornello form   ☒ **D** A rondo   **(1)**

(i) Put a cross in the box next to the statement that is true.

    This excerpt is part of a:

    ☒ **A** Galliard   ☒ **B** Gigue   ☒ **C** Minuet   ☒ **D** Sarabande   **(1)**

(j) Put a cross in the box next to the statement that is true.

    ☒ **A** The excerpt comes from an early Baroque work

    ☒ **B** The excerpt comes from a mid-Baroque work

    ☒ **C** The excerpt comes from a late Baroque work

    ☒ **D** The excerpt comes from an early Classical work   **(1)**

(Total 16 marks)

Question 2   CD 3 Track 11, 2:07–3:39

You will hear an excerpt from *Flow my tears* by Dowland. A skeleton score of this excerpt is provided below. Bar numbers in this question refer to the skeleton score.

(a)   Name the instruments you hear on this recording.

.... **(2)**

(b)   Name the key at bars 1 to 2.

.... **(1)**

(c)   Describe the texture of:

(i)   Bars 4 to 5 (beat 2).

....

(ii)   Bars 5 (beat 3) to 6.

.... **(3)**

(d)   Name the cadence at bars 7 (beat 4) to 8.

.... **(1)**

(e)   How do the first four notes in bar 9 differ from the first four notes in bar 1?

....

.... **(2)**

(f)   Complete the following statement:

In the vocal part, the melodic interval on 'Happie' (bars 12 to 13) is a .... After

this, Dowland extends the melody (at 'happie' in bar 13) by using ....   **(2)**

(g)   In bars 15 to 16, name the key, the type of cadence, and a harmonic device used.

Key: ....

Cadence: ....

Harmonic device: ....   **(3)**

(h)   From what type of song is this excerpt taken?

....   **(1)**

(i)   Put a cross in the box next to the statement that is true.

The overall structure of the song from which this excerpt is taken is:

⊠ **A**   A B A B

⊠ **B**   A A^1 A^2

⊠ **C**   A A B B C C

⊠ **D**   A B C D   **(1)**

(Total 16 marks)

TOTAL FOR SECTION A: 32 MARKS

Section B: Investigating Musical Styles

Question 3

You must answer either (a) INSTRUMENTAL MUSIC or (b) VOCAL MUSIC.

You must answer both part (i) and part (ii) of the question you choose.

(a) INSTRUMENTAL MUSIC

   (i)   Describe the stylistic features of Concerto for Double String Orchestra: movement I by Tippett which reveal an interest in music composed before the 20th century.

(10)

   (ii) Compare and contrast texture and use of instruments in String Quartet in E♭, Op. 33 No. 2, 'The Joke': movement IV by Haydn and in Quartet Op. 22: movement I by Webern.

(18)

OR

(b) VOCAL MUSIC

   (i)   Describe the stylistic features of *Locus iste* by Bruckner which show that this music was composed in the Romantic era.

(10)

   (ii) Compare and contrast the word-setting, vocal melody and rhythm of 'Summertime' from *Porgy and Bess* by Gershwin and *You can get it if you really want* as performed by Desmond Dekker and the Aces.

(18)

(Total 28 marks)

TOTAL FOR SECTION B: 28 MARKS

BLANK PAGE

Section C: Understanding Chords and Lines

Answer both questions.

Question 4

Study the printed music below and answer all the questions that follow.

(a)   Complete the table below. Precisely indicate, using Roman numerals, the chords that are used.

Bar 1: ....I...............

Bar 2: ....

Bar 3, beats 1 to 3: ....   **(2)**

(b)   In bar 6, what kind of non-harmonic note is the quaver C in the right hand of the piano part?

....   **(1)**

(c)   What chord in B♭ major, heard in various inversions and in root position, is used throughout bars 10 and 11?

....   **(1)**

(d)   In what key is the cadence in bars 12 to 13?

....   **(1)**

(e)   What type of chord is used in bar 15?

....   **(1)**

(f)   Complete the sentence below by putting a cross in the box next to the correct answer.

In bar 17 of the right hand of the piano part, the note B♭ is:

☒ **A** An anticipation

☒ **B** An auxiliary note

☒ **C** A passing note

☒ **D** A suspension   **(1)**

(g)   Name the harmonic device used from bar 20 to bar 22 beat 1.

....   **(1)**

(Total 8 marks)

Question 5

Complete the music below for SATB voices in short score choosing suitable chords. Some credit will be given for the appropriate use of non-harmonic notes. You may use manuscript paper for rough work, but you must write your answer on the score below.

(Total 12 marks)

TOTAL FOR PART C: 20 MARKS

TOTAL FOR PAPER: 80 MARKS

END OF PAPER

Test paper for 2012

The test paper below has questions for all three sections of Unit 3. Answer all questions, but note that there is a choice in Question 3, where you can answer on the area of study Instrumental Music or on the area of study Vocal Music.

Allow yourself 5 minutes' reading time before starting work on the paper. The two hours allowed to complete the test paper must start after the 5 minutes have been used up.

The Section A questions (Questions 1 and 2) together should take between 25 and 30 minutes, including the timed pauses. If possible, someone other than yourself should operate the CD player and time the pauses – you will have enough to do with listening to the music and answering the questions! The timing of pauses is shown on page 9 of the main book.

Keep an eye on the clock as you work through Sections B and C. In Section B you must work from memory, and not use a copy of the anthology. You need not quote bar numbers, unless they easily come to mind – but try to give examples of at least some points, noting for example that a long dominant pedal occurs 'near the end'. For Question 5 only, you can check your work on a piano or keyboard (use headphones if other students are working the paper at the same time as you).

Section A: Listening

Answer both questions.

Question 1   **CD 2 Track 15, 0:33–1:40**

You will hear an excerpt from *Kinderscenen*, Op. 15 No. 11 by Schumann. A skeleton score of this excerpt is provided below. Bar numbers in this question refer to the skeleton score.

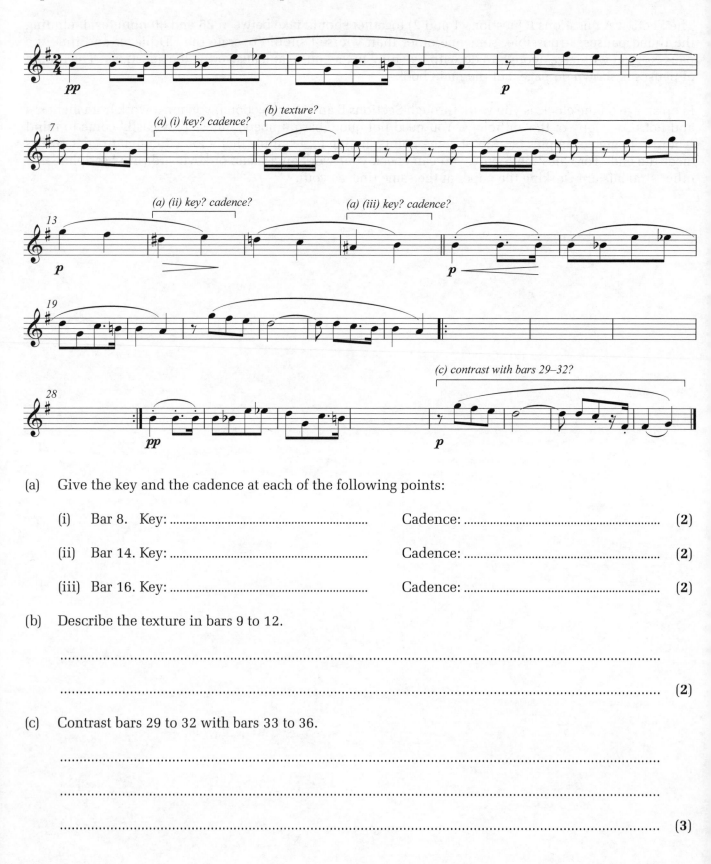

(a) Give the key and the cadence at each of the following points:

    (i) Bar 8. Key: .... Cadence: .... **(2)**

    (ii) Bar 14. Key: .... Cadence: .... **(2)**

    (iii) Bar 16. Key: .... Cadence: .... **(2)**

(b) Describe the texture in bars 9 to 12.

....

.... **(2)**

(c) Contrast bars 29 to 32 with bars 33 to 36.

....

....

.... **(3)**

(d)   Describe those features of the excerpt which justify the title 'Frightening'.

....

....

....   **(3)**

(e)   Put a cross in the box next to the statement that is true.

The type of piece from which this excerpt is taken is best described as:

☒ **A** Gigue

☒ **B** March

☒ **C** Romantic miniature

☒ **D** Saltarello   **(1)**

(f)   Put a cross in the box next to the statement that is true.

The overall structure of the movement from which this excerpt is taken is:

☒ **A** Rondo

☒ **B** Rounded binary

☒ **C** Sonata form

☒ **D** Ternary   **(1)**

(Total 16 marks)

Question 2   CD 4 Track 11, 2:14–2:58

You will hear an excerpt from *Honey Don't* by Carl Perkins. A skeleton score of this excerpt is provided below. Bar numbers in this question refer to the skeleton score.

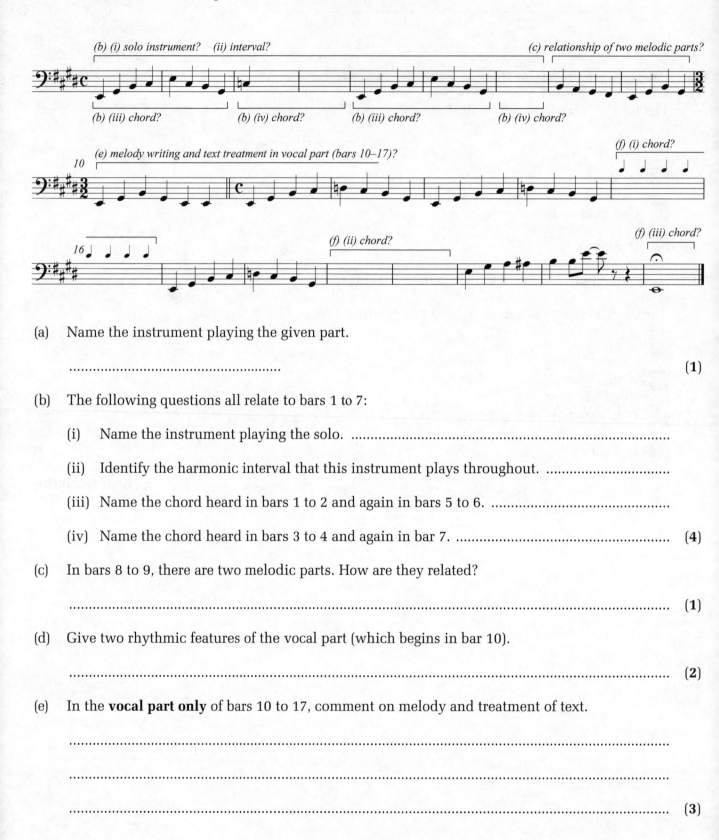

(a)   Name the instrument playing the given part.

      ....   **(1)**

(b)   The following questions all relate to bars 1 to 7:

      (i)   Name the instrument playing the solo. ....

      (ii)   Identify the harmonic interval that this instrument plays throughout. ....

      (iii) Name the chord heard in bars 1 to 2 and again in bars 5 to 6. ....

      (iv)   Name the chord heard in bars 3 to 4 and again in bar 7. .... **(4)**

(c)   In bars 8 to 9, there are two melodic parts. How are they related?

      .... **(1)**

(d)   Give two rhythmic features of the vocal part (which begins in bar 10).

      .... **(2)**

(e)   In the **vocal part only** of bars 10 to 17, comment on melody and treatment of text.

      ....

      ....

      .... **(3)**

(f) Name the chords in:

    (i) Bars 15 to 16: ....

    (ii) Bars 19 to 20: ....

    (iii) Bar 23: .... **(3)**

(g) Put a cross in the box next to the statement that best describes the structure of the piece from which this excerpt is taken.

    ☒ **A** Sixteen-bar blues

    ☒ **B** Twelve-bar blues

    ☒ **C** Through-composed

    ☒ **D** Verse and chorus **(1)**

(h) Put a cross in the box next to the statement that best describes the style of the music.

    ☒ **A** Bebop

    ☒ **B** Reggae

    ☒ **C** Rhythm and blues

    ☒ **D** Rockabilly **(1)**

(Total 16 marks)

TOTAL FOR SECTION A: 32 MARKS

Section B: Investigating Musical Styles

Question 3

You must answer either (a) INSTRUMENTAL MUSIC or (b) VOCAL MUSIC.

You must answer both part (i) and part (ii) of the question you choose.

(a)   INSTRUMENTAL MUSIC

   (i)   Describe the stylistic features of Trio Sonata in D, Op. 3 No. 2: movement IV by Corelli which show that this music was composed in the Baroque era.

(10)

   (ii)   Compare and contrast the melody and harmony of *Harold in Italy: movement I* by Berlioz and Septet in E♭, Op. 20: movement I by Beethoven.

(**18**)

OR

(b)   VOCAL MUSIC

   (i)   Describe the stylistic features of *My mother bids me bind my hair* by Haydn which show that this music was composed in the Classical era.

(**10**)

   (ii)   Compare and contrast the structure and tonality of *Sing we at pleasure* by Weelkes and *A Day in the Life* by the Beatles.

(**18**)

(**Total 28 marks**)

TOTAL FOR SECTION B: 28 MARKS

BLANK PAGE

Section C: Understanding Chords and Lines

Answer both questions.

Question 4

Study the printed music below and answer all the questions that follow.

Ein bisschen aus der Nase (*literally* 'A bit through the nose' – i.e. with a rather nasal tone)

(a) Complete the table below. Precisely indicate, using Roman numerals, the chords that are used at:

Bar 1, quaver beat 3: ....I...................

Bar 1, quaver beat 4: ....

Bar 2, quaver beats 1 and 3: ....

Bar 2, quaver beat 4: .... **(3)**

(b) Identify the key at:

Bars 6 to 7 (crotchet beat 1): ....

Bars 8 to 9: .... **(2)**

(c) What type of cadence is used in bars 14 to 15?

.... **(1)**

(d) What type of non-harmonic note is the demisemiquaver E at the end of bar 20 (vocal part)?

.... **(1)**

(e) Complete the sentence below by putting a cross in the box next to the correct answer.

The A♯ at the beginning of bar 24 is:

☒ **A** A chromatic appoggiatura

☒ **B** A chromatic passing note

☒ **C** An échappée (escape note)

☒ **D** A lower auxiliary note **(1)**

(Total 8 marks)

Question 5

Complete the music below for SATB voices in short score choosing suitable chords. Some credit will be given for the appropriate use of non-harmonic notes. You may use manuscript paper for rough work, but you must write your answer on the score below.

(Total 12 marks)

TOTAL FOR PART C: 20 MARKS

TOTAL FOR PAPER: 80 MARKS

END OF PAPER

Test paper for 2013

The test paper below has questions for all three sections of Unit 3. Answer all questions, but note that there is a choice in Question 3, where you can answer on the area of study Instrumental Music or on the area of study Vocal Music.

Allow yourself 5 minutes' reading time before starting work on the paper. The two hours allowed to complete the test paper must start after the 5 minutes have been used up.

The Section A questions (Questions 1 and 2) together should take between 25 and 30 minutes, including the timed pauses. If possible, someone other than yourself should operate the CD player and time the pauses – you will have enough to do with listening to the music and answering the questions! The timing of pauses is shown on page 9 of the main book.

Keep an eye on the clock as you work through Sections B and C. In Section B you must work from memory, and not use a copy of the anthology. You need not quote bar numbers, unless they easily come to mind – but try to give examples of at least some points, noting for example that a long dominant pedal occurs 'near the end'. For Question 5 only, you can check your work on a piano or keyboard (use headphones if other students are working the paper at the same time as you).

Section A: Listening

Answer both questions.

Question 1   **CD 2 Track 12, 4:02–5:09**

You will hear an excerpt from the first movement of Sonata in B♭, K. 333 by Mozart. A skeleton score of this excerpt is provided below. Bar numbers in this question refer to the skeleton score.

(a)   Compare the melody from bar 2 (beat 4) to bar 4 (beat 2) with that of the preceding two bars.

.... (1)

(b) Complete the following sentences.

The chord in bar 6 is a .... chord which leads in bar 7 to an F major tonic chord

in .... inversion. The chord on the last quaver of bar 7 is chord .... and

it is part of a(n) .... cadence.   **(4)**

(c) Name the key into which the music suddenly moves at bar 8.

....   **(1)**

(d) Describe the texture used in bars 8 to 17.

....

....   **(2)**

(e) Name the rhythmic device used in the melody at bars 10 to 11.

....   **(1)**

(f) Name the key and cadence at bars 17 (beat 4) to 18 (beat 1).

Key: ....

Cadence: ....   **(2)**

(g) In bars 24 to 30, do the chords change more or less frequently than previously?

....   **(1)**

(h) Complete the following statements.

In bar 31, the music is in the key of ...., and the dissonance on beat 1 of bar 32 is

a(n) .... The dissonance on beat 1 of bar 34 is a(n) ....   **(3)**

(i) Put a cross in the box next to the statement that is true.

☒ **A** This excerpt forms the exposition section

☒ **B** This excerpt is the bridge passage

☒ **C** This excerpt is the entire development and opening bars of the recapitulation

☒ **D** This excerpt is the recapitulation

(1)

(Total 16 marks)

Question 2   **CD 3 Track 11, 2:07–3:39**

You will hear an excerpt from *Flow my tears* by Dowland. A skeleton score of this excerpt is provided below. Bar numbers in this question refer to the skeleton score.

(a)   Name the instruments you hear on this recording.

.... **(2)**

(b)   Name the key at bars 1 to 2.

.... **(1)**

(c)   Describe the texture of:

(i)   Bars 4 to 5 (beat 2).

....

(ii)   Bars 5 (beat 3) to 6.

.... **(3)**

(d)   Name the cadence at bars 7 (beat 4) to 8.

.... **(1)**

(e)   How do the first four notes in bar 9 differ from the first four notes in bar 1?

....

.... **(2)**

(f)   Complete the following statement:

   In the vocal part, the melodic interval on 'Happie' (bars 12 to 13) is a .... After

   this, Dowland extends the melody (at 'happie' in bar 13) by using .... **(2)**

(g)   In bars 15 to 16, name the key, the type of cadence, and a harmonic device used.

   Key: ....

   Cadence: ....

   Harmonic device: ....   **(3)**

(h)   From what type of song is this excerpt taken?

   ....   **(1)**

(i)   Put a cross in the box next to the statement that is true.

   The overall structure of the song from which this excerpt is taken is:

   ☒ **A**   A B A B

   ☒ **B**   A A¹ A²

   ☒ **C**   A A B B C C

   ☒ **D**   A B C D   **(1)**

(Total 16 marks)

TOTAL FOR SECTION A: 32 MARKS

Section B: Investigating Musical Styles

Question 3

You must answer either (a) INSTRUMENTAL MUSIC or (b) VOCAL MUSIC.

You must answer both part (i) and part (ii) of the question you choose.

(a)   INSTRUMENTAL MUSIC

    (i)   Describe the stylistic features of *Prélude à l'après-midi d'un faune* by Debussy which show that this music was the work of an impressionist composer.

(10)

    (ii)   (ii) Compare and contrast the texture and tonality of *New York Counterpoint: movement II* by Reich and Sonata for Horn, Trumpet and Trombone: movement I by Poulenc.

(18)

OR

(b)   VOCAL MUSIC

    (i)   Describe the stylistic features of *Ohimè, se tanto amate* by Monteverdi which show that this music is the work of an early Baroque composer.

(10)

    (ii)   Compare and contrast the word-setting, rhythm and metre of *The Lamb* by Tavener and *Tupelo Honey* by Van Morrison.

(18)

(Total 28 marks)

TOTAL FOR SECTION B: 28 MARKS

BLANK PAGE

Section C: Understanding Chords and Lines

Answer both questions.

Question 4

Study the printed music below and answer all the questions that follow.

(a)   What type of cadence is used in bars 1 to 2?

        ....   (1)

(b)   Complete the table below. Precisely indicate, using Roman numerals, the chords that are used at:

   Bar 3, beats 1 to 2: ....I............

   Bar 3 beats, 3 to 4: ....

   Bar 4, beat 1: ....

   Bar 4, beat 2: ....   (3)

(c) What type of non-harmonic note is the quaver G at the end of bar 6 (piano, left-hand part)?

.... **(1)**

(d) Identify the key in bar 10, beats 2 to 4.

.... **(1)**

(e) What chord is used at bar 12, beat 3?

.... **(1)**

(f) What type of cadence is used in bars 14 to 15?

.... **(1)**

(Total 8 marks)

Question 5

Complete the music below for SATB voices in short score choosing suitable chords. Some credit will be given for the appropriate use of non-harmonic notes. You may use manuscript paper for rough work, but you must write your answer on the score below.

(Total 12 marks)

TOTAL FOR PART C: 20 MARKS

TOTAL FOR PAPER: 80 MARKS

END OF PAPER

(e) Describe the instrumental techniques employed in the printed part in bars 11 and 12.

....

.... (2)

(f) Describe the roles of the voice and of the instruments in bars 15 to 18.

....

....

.... (3)

(g) Complete the following table of chords:

Bar 17: ....G.............

Bar 19: ....

Bar 21: ....

Bar 23: .... (3)

(h) Describe the way the quavers in the printed part in bar 25 are performed rhythmically.

.... (1)

(i) Put a cross in the box next to the statement that is true.

☒ A This excerpt is taken from an example of reggae

☒ B This excerpt is taken from an example of rhythm and blues

☒ C This excerpt is taken from an example of rocksteady

☒ D This excerpt is taken from an example of electric folk (1)

(j) Put a cross in the box next to the statement that is true.

☒ A The overall structure of the song from which this excerpt is taken is binary

☒ B The overall structure of the song from which this excerpt is taken is ternary

☒ C The overall structure of the song from which this excerpt is taken is strophic

☒ D The overall structure of the song from which this excerpt is taken is 16-bar popular song form (1)

(Total 16 marks)

2013 Test 5

You will hear an excerpt from the second movement of *New York Counterpoint* by Reich. A skeleton score of this excerpt is provided below. Bar numbers in this question refer to the skeleton score.

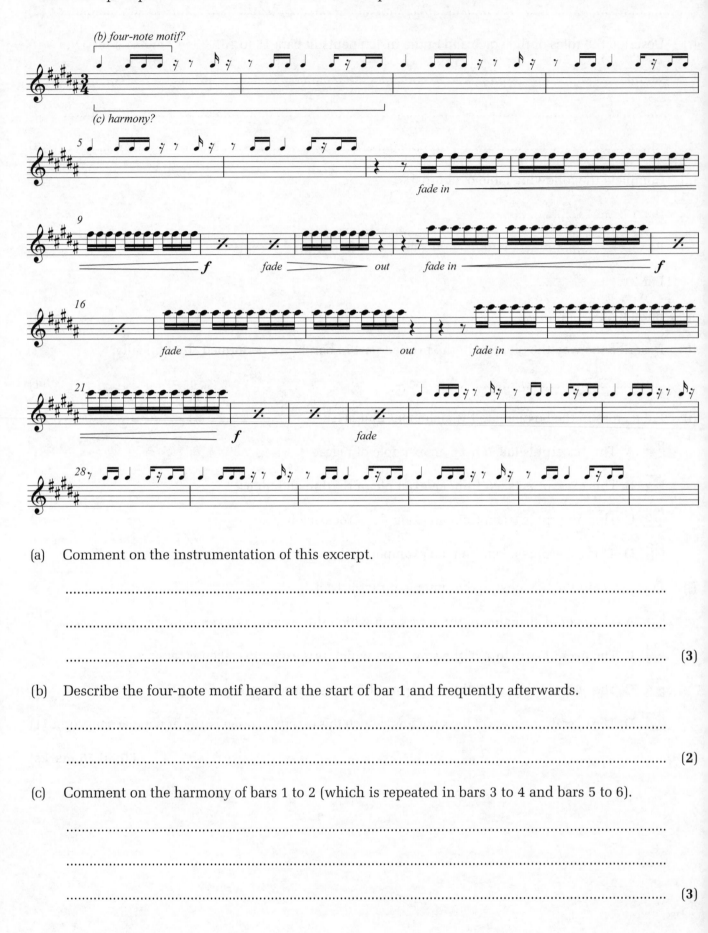

(a)   Comment on the instrumentation of this excerpt.

....

....

....   **(3)**

(b)   Describe the four-note motif heard at the start of bar 1 and frequently afterwards.

....

....   **(2)**

(c)   Comment on the harmony of bars 1 to 2 (which is repeated in bars 3 to 4 and bars 5 to 6).

....

....

....   **(3)**

(d) Describe how Reich expands upon this opening harmonic scheme beginning from bar 7.

....

.... (2)

(e) Describe the textures you hear in this excerpt.

....

....

....

.... (4)

(f) Put a cross in the box next to the statement that is true.

The work from which this excerpt is taken is best described as:

☒ **A** Aleatoric   ☒ **B** Avant-garde   ☒ **C** Minimalist   ☒ **D** Serial   (1)

(g) Put a cross in the box next to the year in which this music was composed.

☒ **A** 1945   ☒ **B** 1965   ☒ **C** 1985   ☒ **D** 2005   (1)

(Total 16 marks)

2013 Test 6

You will hear an excerpt from *The Lamb* by John Tavener. A skeleton score of this excerpt is provided below. Bar numbers in this question refer to the skeleton score.

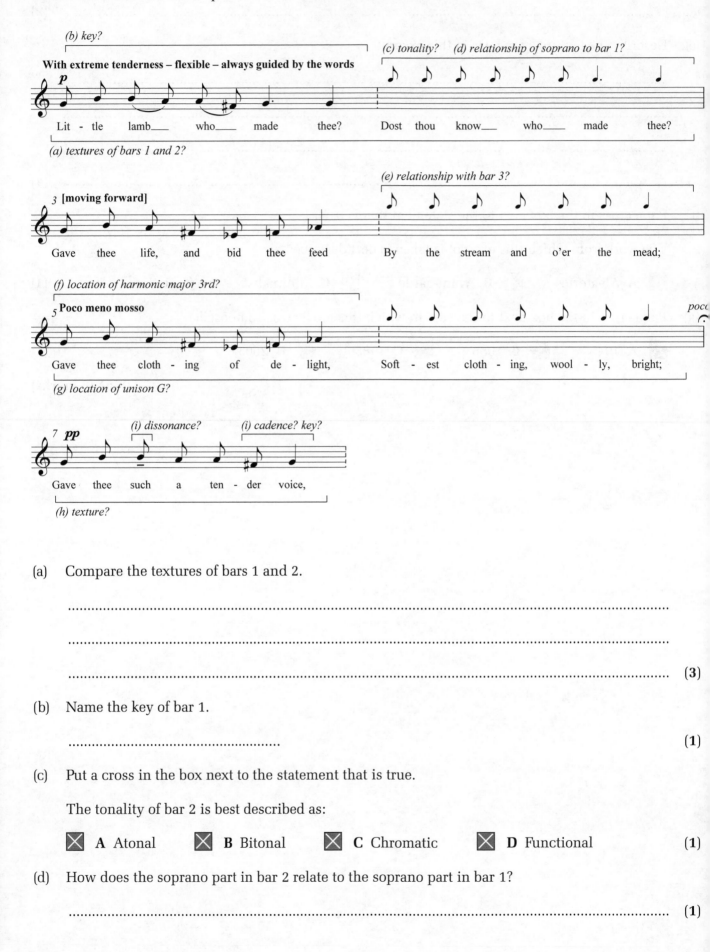

(a) Compare the textures of bars 1 and 2.

....

....

.... **(3)**

(b) Name the key of bar 1.

.... **(1)**

(c) Put a cross in the box next to the statement that is true.

The tonality of bar 2 is best described as:

☒ **A** Atonal   ☒ **B** Bitonal   ☒ **C** Chromatic   ☒ **D** Functional   **(1)**

(d) How does the soprano part in bar 2 relate to the soprano part in bar 1?

.... **(1)**

(e) How does the given part in bar 4 relate to bar 3?

.... **(1)**

(f) A harmonic* major third can be heard in bar 5. Identify its location by saying on which quaver of the bar it comes (e.g. first, second, third, etc.).

.... **(1)**

* Harmonic intervals occur when the notes sound together, rather than one after the other (melodic).

(g) In bars 5 to 6, there is a unison G on the word 'Gave'. On what other word do you hear the same interval?

.... **(1)**

(h) Describe the texture of bar 7.

.... **(2)**

(i) Complete the following statements.

The dissonance in the soprano on the third quaver of bar 7 is a(n) ....

The final cadence is .... and the key is .... **(4)**

(j) Put a cross in the box next to the statement that is true.

☒ **A** The excerpt is taken from an anthem

☒ **B** The excerpt is taken from a chorale

☒ **C** The excerpt is taken from a madrigal

☒ **D** The excerpt is taken from a motet **(1)**

(Total 16 marks)

2013 Test 7   **CD 2 Track 12, 0:00–1:00**

You will hear an excerpt from the first movement of Sonata in B♭, K. 333 by Mozart. A skeleton score of this excerpt is provided below. Bar numbers in this question refer to the skeleton score.

(a)   An ornament symbol has been omitted from the skeleton score right at the start of the excerpt. Insert it in the stave below:

(1)

(b)   Describe the texture of bars 1 to 4, including the number of parts involved.

....

.... (2)

(c)　Name the rhythmic device in the upper part of bar 5.

　　　　... **(1)**

(d)　Comment on the chord progression and dissonance treatment from bar 9 (beat 3) to bar 10 (beat 3).

　　　　..

　　　　..

　　　　.. **(4)**

(e)　Name the type of dissonance used on the first crotchet beat of bar 12.

　　　　... **(1)**

(f)　Complete the following sentence.

　　　　In bars 21 to 22, there is a(n) .... cadence in the key of .... **(2)**

(g)　What one word best describes the texture in bars 24 to 25?

　　　　... **(1)**

(h)　Name the compositional device used in bars 27 to 28.

　　　　... **(1)**

(i)　Contrast bar 31 with bar 23.

　　　　.. **(1)**

(j)　Put a cross in the box next to the statement that is true.

　　　　The overall structure of the piece from which this excerpt is taken is:

　　　　☒ **A** Binary form　　☒ **B** Sonata form　　☒ **C** Ritornello form　　☒ **D** Rondo form　　**(1)**

(k)　Put a cross in the box next to the statement that is true.

　　　　☒ **A** This excerpt comes from a Baroque work

　　　　☒ **B** This excerpt comes from a Classical work

　　　　☒ **C** This excerpt comes from an early Romantic work

　　　　☒ **D** This excerpt comes from a late Romantic work　　**(1)**

(Total 16 marks)

2013 Test 8   CD 4 Track 14, 2:06–2:58

You will hear an excerpt from *Tupelo Honey* by Van Morrison. A skeleton score of this excerpt is provided below. Bar numbers in this question refer to the skeleton score.

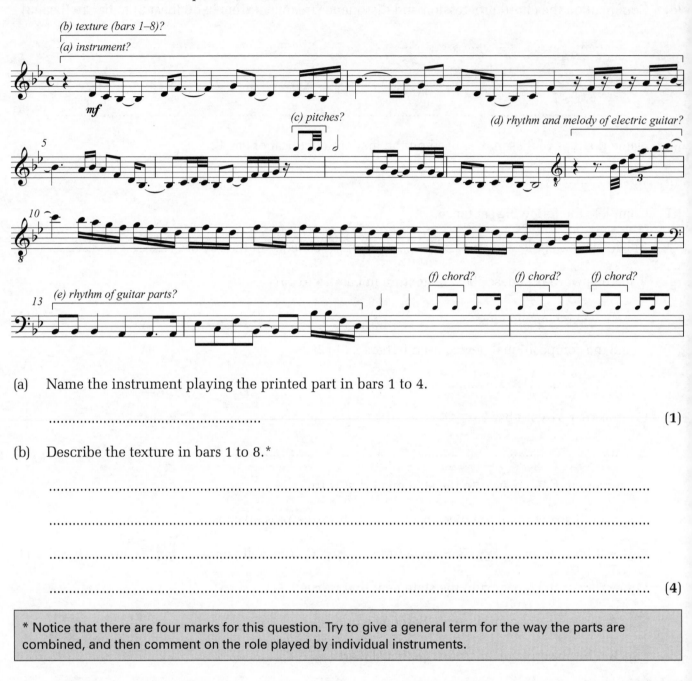

(a)   Name the instrument playing the printed part in bars 1 to 4.

....   **(1)**

(b)   Describe the texture in bars 1 to 8.*

....

....

....

.... **(4)**

> * Notice that there are four marks for this question. Try to give a general term for the way the parts are combined, and then comment on the role played by individual instruments.

(c)   Three pitches have been omitted from the given melody line in bar 6. Insert them on the stave below, using the rhythm given:

                                                                                                          (3)

(d)   In bar 9, the acoustic guitar part is given. Comment on the rhythm and melody of the **electric** guitar in this bar.

....

.... **(2)**

(e) Comment on the rhythm of the electric and acoustic guitar parts in bars 13 to 14.

....

.... **(2)**

(f) Complete the following table of chords:

Bar 15, beat 1: ....Bb..........

Bar 15, beat 3: ....

Bar 16, beat 1: ....

Bar 16, beat 3: .... **(3)**

(g) Put a cross in the box next to the statement that is true.

⊠ **A** This excerpt is the bridge

⊠ **B** This excerpt is the instrumental

⊠ **C** This excerpt is the middle eight

⊠ **D** This excerpt is the chorus **(1)**

(Total 16 marks)

2013 Test 9   **CD 2 Track 8, 1:38–2:32**

You will hear an excerpt from the first movement of the Sonata for Horn, Trumpet and Trombone by Poulenc. A skeleton score of this excerpt is provided below. Bar numbers in this question refer to the skeleton score.

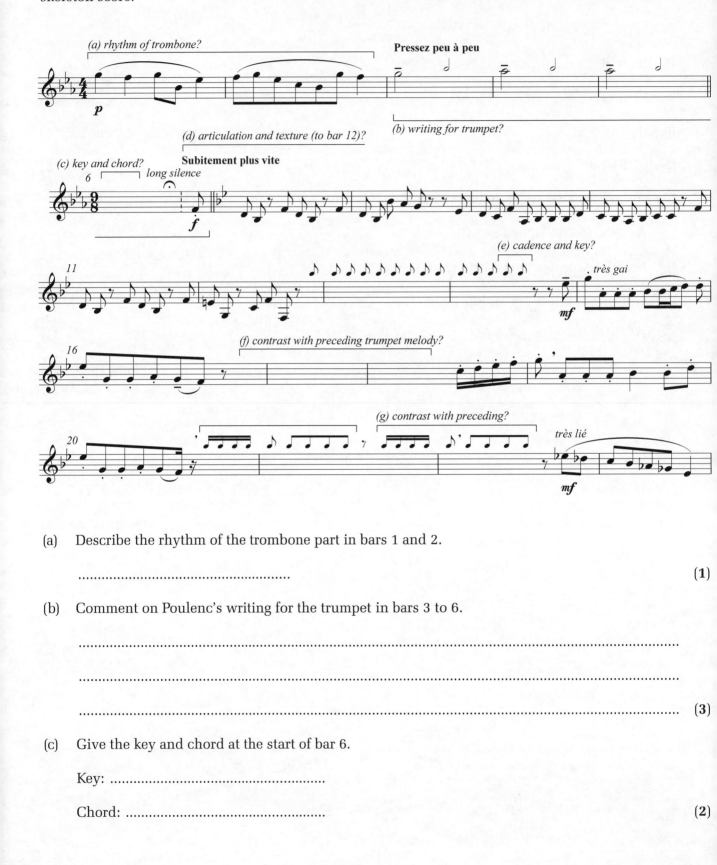

(a)   Describe the rhythm of the trombone part in bars 1 and 2.

       ....   **(1)**

(b)   Comment on Poulenc's writing for the trumpet in bars 3 to 6.

       ....

       ....

       .... **(3)**

(c)   Give the key and chord at the start of bar 6.

       Key: ....

       Chord: ....   **(2)**

(d)   Comment on the articulation and texture of bars 6 (last quaver) to 12.

....

....

.... **(3)**

(e)   Complete the following sentence:

At bar 14 there is a(n) .... cadence in the key of .... **(2)**

(f)   How does the trumpet melody of bars 16 (last quaver) to bar 18 differ from the trumpet melody of bars 14 (last quaver) to 16?

....

.... **(2)**

(g)   How do bars 21 (beat 4) to 22 (beat 3) differ from bars 20 (beat 4) to 21 (beat 3)?

....

.... **(2)**

(h)   Put a cross in the box next to the statement that is true.

☒ **A** This excerpt comes from the development section

☒ **B** This excerpt comes from the end of the central section of the movement

☒ **C** This excerpt leads into the coda

☒ **D** This excerpt is a trio section   **(1)**

(Total 16 marks)

2013 Test 10   **CD 3 Track 13, 1:37–2:42**

You will hear an excerpt from *Ohimè, se tanto amate* by Monteverdi. A skeleton score of this excerpt is provided below. Bar numbers in this question refer to the skeleton score.

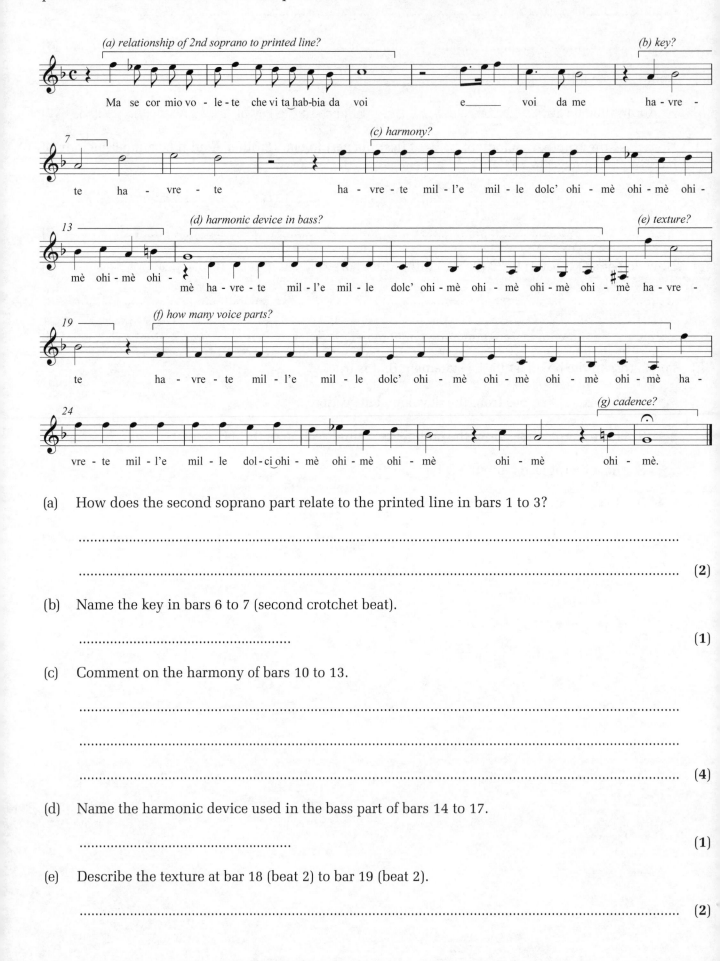

(a)   How does the second soprano part relate to the printed line in bars 1 to 3?

    ....

    .... **(2)**

(b)   Name the key in bars 6 to 7 (second crotchet beat).

    .... **(1)**

(c)   Comment on the harmony of bars 10 to 13.

    ....

    ....

    .... **(4)**

(d)   Name the harmonic device used in the bass part of bars 14 to 17.

    .... **(1)**

(e)   Describe the texture at bar 18 (beat 2) to bar 19 (beat 2).

    .... **(2)**

(f) How many voice parts do you hear in bars 19 (beat 4) to 23 (beat 3)?

.... **(1)**

(g) Comment on the cadence at bars 28 (beat 4) to 29.

....

.... **(2)**

(h) Mention some devices, not previously referred to, which help to emphasise the meaning of the text.

....

.... **(2)**

(i) Put a cross in the box next to the statement that is true.

This excerpt comes from a work which is an example of:

☒ **A** Early Renaissance style

☒ **B** Prima prattica

☒ **C** Seconda prattica

☒ **D** Late Baroque style **(1)**

(Total 16 marks)

2013 Test 11   **CD 4 Track 14, 0:00–1:10**

You will hear an excerpt from *Tupelo Honey* by Van Morrison. A skeleton score of this excerpt is provided below. Bar numbers in this question refer to the skeleton score.

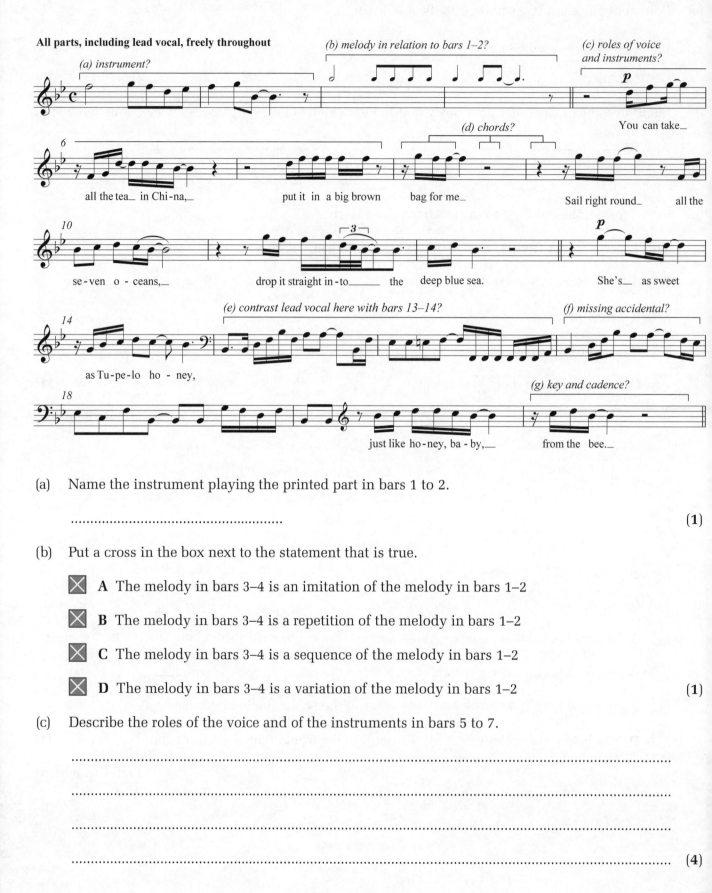

(a)   Name the instrument playing the printed part in bars 1 to 2.

    ....   **(1)**

(b)   Put a cross in the box next to the statement that is true.

    ☒ **A** The melody in bars 3–4 is an imitation of the melody in bars 1–2

    ☒ **B** The melody in bars 3–4 is a repetition of the melody in bars 1–2

    ☒ **C** The melody in bars 3–4 is a sequence of the melody in bars 1–2

    ☒ **D** The melody in bars 3–4 is a variation of the melody in bars 1–2   **(1)**

(c)   Describe the roles of the voice and of the instruments in bars 5 to 7.

    ....

    ....

    ....

    .... **(4)**

(d)   Complete the following table of chords:*

Bar 7, beat 1: ....B♭.........

Bar 7, beat 3: ....Dm/A.........

Bar 8, beat 1: ....

Bar 8, beat 3: ....

Bar 9, beat 1: ....   (3)

> * In questions on popular music and jazz, chords are best described using chord symbols (Em, G⁷, etc.), as the table above makes clear. Notice how the given chords for bar 7 'set the scene' and help you put bar 8 in its harmonic context.

(e)   How does the melody in the lead vocal in bars 15 to 16 differ from the given lead vocal melody in bars 13 to 14?

....

....

.... (3)

(f)   An accidental has been missed out in bar 17. Insert it at the appropriate point in the stave below:

(1)

(g)   Name the key and cadence in bar 20.

Key: ....

Cadence: ....   (2)

(h)   Put a cross in the box next to the statement that is true.

☒ A The lead vocal melody uses all the notes in the major scale throughout

☒ B The lead vocal melody uses all the notes in the minor scale throughout

☒ C The lead vocal melody uses all the notes in the pentatonic scale throughout

☒ D The lead vocal melody uses all the notes in the whole-tone scale throughout   (1)

(Total 16 marks)

How to find and invent more questions for Unit 3

Teachers: here are some hints on finding and inventing practice material in addition to the questions provided in this book.

> *Special note for students*: if you make up questions yourself, ask your teacher to check them, particularly to ensure that they are at a suitable level of difficulty. Also ask your teacher to mark or help you mark the answers – assessing answers well can be harder than writing good questions!

1. **Past examination papers.** For Section C, use the questions in the Edexcel Unit 3 examination papers for 2009 and 2010 (and other years as they become available). The syllabus requirements for Section C are the same for the years 2011–2013 as they were for 2009–2010.

   Because the lists of set works *do* change, Section A and B questions from past Edexcel papers are not usable again – except where particular set works return. For example, Stravinsky's *Symphony of Psalms: movement III* was set in 2009 and is also in the list for 2012 (see pages 59–60 of the specification).

2. **Edexcel's Sample Assessment Materials** (available to download from the Edexcel website) were designed to prepare teachers and students for the 2009 exam in particular. Section C questions may be used in preparation for the 2011–2013 exams, but Section A and B questions will be relevant only where particular set works for 2009 recur.

3. **Other Rhinegold Education publications.** Additional teaching and practice material for Section C, and some tests, are published in the *AS Harmony Workbook*. There are also Section C tests in the present authors' *Edexcel AS Music Listening Tests* (2nd edition, for the years 2009 and 2010). For additional material on Section B, see the *AS Revision Guide (2nd edition)*, and the *Edexcel AS Music Study Guide (2nd edition)*.

4. **Inventing new questions.** Begin by finding out what the specification requires for the relevant examination year. Take full advantage of the various guidance materials that Edexcel provides on its website, notably the Tutor Support Materials.

Inventing questions for Section B

Section B is the easiest to write questions for, so we'll take this first.

➤ Look at pages 59–61 of the specification to identify the set works for the year of your AS exam.
➤ Choose between the areas of study Instrumental Music and Vocal Music. (In the exam students have to answer on one area only.)

Ten-mark questions

➤ Pick any work from the chosen area of study.
➤ A 10-mark question must require this work to be related to its historical or cultural context.* It may well be similar in format to the following: 'What musical features of *composer a*'s *work b* indicate that it was composed in the *c period*?'

> * As explained in the specification (page 62, section 3), and in 'Getting Started September 2007' (Tutor Support Materials), page 28.

➤ Check that the question is broadly comparable to the 10-mark 'part (i)' questions in the test-paper insert.

Eighteen-mark questions

➢ Pick any *two* works from the chosen area of study.
➢ An 18-mark question must ask for comparison and contrast of two musical features in the two selected works.* It may well be similar in format to the following: 'Compare and contrast *feature a* and *feature b* in *work c* and *work d*.'

---

* As explained in the specification (page 62, section 3), and in 'Getting Started September 2007' (Tutor Support Materials). Page 28 provides a list of the kinds of features that could be asked about.

➢ In the exam, the two works that feature in the part (ii) question will be different from the single work referred to in the part (i) question.

Inventing questions for Section C

Practice material for analysis questions

➢ To invent a specimen question, find a piece for single voice and keyboard, notated on three staves.
➢ The music is best taken from 18th- or early 19th-century repertoires (Baroque, Classical or early Romantic). Later music usually has chords that the specification does not require students to identify; most earlier music does not use the necessary kind of simple functional harmony.
➢ Take an extract, lasting 10–20 bars or a little more (depending partly on the length of the bars).
➢ Study carefully the layout of the questions asked in past papers and the types of questions asked.
➢ Ask for eight pieces of information (each worth one mark). Some of these must require the labelling of chords with roman numerals (and inversion letters if necessary). Note that a model answer should be given first (e.g. indicate that bar 1 beat 1 = chord I), partly to help identify the key.
➢ Other questions can involve recognising types of non-chord note (e.g. passing notes, suspensions or anticipations), cadences, or keys. Check on the expected 'harmonic and tonal vocabulary' in the specification (page 58, section 4).
➢ It is not always necessary to go to the trouble of inventing whole analysis questions or working with music on three staves. It is always useful to identify keys, chords, cadences and non-chord notes in hymn tunes and chorales – or indeed in any music being prepared for performance.

Practice material for the SATB harmony question

Phrases from hymn tunes and chorales can provide useful practice. Copy out the whole melody for your students, together with the alto, tenor and bass parts for all but the final five beats of the melody. Students must then supply the missing parts, beginning with the bass part.

If hymn tunes are used, it's best to work with those composed in the 18th and 19th centuries. Avoid choosing phrases that appear to have chromatic notes, or to modulate. Often the first or the last phrase of a hymn will be most suitable for Unit 3 practice.

If phrases from chorales are chosen, students are not obliged to reproduce the characteristics of Bach's often rather elaborate style of harmonisation – something simpler is perfectly in order.

Inventing questions for Section A

➢ Find out what are the set works for the year of your AS exam (see pages 59–61 of the specification).
➢ In the exam students need to answer one question on each area of study, so it is wise to cover both areas with equal thoroughness.
➢ Take any set work, and choose any passage that lasts for a minute or slightly more.
➢ Decide on a number of things that could reasonably be answered, given what you expect your students to know at the time you invent the test, and the five hearings of the chosen passage that they will get in the exam.
➢ Questions might be asked, for example, about the texture of particular passages, instrumentation, or

the character and development of melodic motifs – or about keys, cadences and chords, or form.

➢ Look at the tests on pages 9–63, and at past exam papers, for further detail. Questions must be designed to require short responses (often one or two lines, but sometimes just single words, or a letter in response to a multiple-choice item).

➢ In the exam there may be ten or more parts to a Section A question, with 16 marks in total. Some questions are worth one mark; most others carry two or three marks.

➢ A skeleton score must be provided to guide students as they go through the excerpt. This usually shows a slightly incomplete version of the main melody part, designed not to give away the answers. For example, if the desired answer to a question on bars 3–4 is 'sequence', the skeleton score must not show the notes E–F–G–A in bar 3 and D–E–F–G in bar 4. Bracketed cues are given to indicate the bars to which particular questions refer. Look at past papers and tests in this book to see more clearly how skeleton scores are constructed.

Answers and how to mark them

Note that, in the following mark schemes, letters, words or phrases in parentheses are not essential: for example 'pizz(icato)' means that you get the mark for 'pizzicato' in full or for the abbreviation 'pizz.'. Numbers in parentheses are numbers of marks to be awarded. An oblique stroke (/) separates alternative correct solutions. Letters, words or phrases which are <u>underlined</u> are essential: you don't get the mark without them.

If you ever provide *correct and relevant* information that is not listed below – for no mark scheme is completely comprehensive – you can receive credit for this. Ask your teacher if you are in doubt.

Section A: 2011

2011 Test 1

Based on Edexcel Anthology No. 57 (p. 509), bars 33–52.

(a) (i) changes to (F) minor (with sixth and seventh) (1)/Fm⁷ (1) (accept Fm); (ii) C (major) (1)

(b) pentatonic (1)

(c) It uses just three notes/GAC (1) from the pentatonic scale (previously used) (1), played repetitively (1) in continuous semiquavers (except for a final quaver) (1), so producing a cross-rhythmic effect (1). Max. (3).

(d) Crotchet/single/opening chord (1) of G (1) with drum fill (1) involving semiquavers (1) and sextuplet (semiquaver) groups (accept instead triplets) (1). Max. (3).

(e) G (major) (1); A minor/Am (1); E (major) (1)

(f) Bar 16 (beat 4) opens with an octave leap (1) (whereas bar 13 opens with top G). The four-quaver rhythm in bar 13 (1) is replaced with crotchet and two quavers (1), leading to delayed G (1) and a leap of a 3rd (1) instead of stepwise movement (1). Max. (3).

(g) C (1)

(h) Britpop (1)

2011 Test 2

Based on Edexcel Anthology No. 30 (p. 305), bars 21–48.

(a) (i) monophonic at bar 1 (1); then three parts (1), without bass (1); imitation (1) by inversion (1). Max. (3). (ii) four part (1) homophonic/(mostly) homorhythmic/chordal (1).

(b) C major (1); imperfect (1)

(c) appoggiatura (1)

(d) G major (1)

(e) V⁷c (1) (allow the somewhat similar-sounding VIIb); I (1); IV (1)

(f) suspension (1)

(g) perfect (1)

(h) D (1)

(i) D (1)

2011 Test 3

Based on Edexcel Anthology No. 16 (p. 202), bars 99–172.

(a) perfect (1)

(b) tonic (1) pedal (1)

(c) Three parts (to start with) (1), then four (1); (some impression of) counterpoint (1); parallel 3rds (between violin II and viola II and viola and cello) (1); violins in octaves (some of the time) (1); inverted (dominant) pedal (violin I) (1). Max. (3). *Note*: (i) the word 'pedal' appears in the answers to both part (b) on harmony and part (c) on texture, because it is possible to regard pedals as both harmonic and textural features; (ii) although there is some impression of counterpoint, with a melodic idea passed between the parts, this is not strictly 'imitation' – there is no overlapping between one entry and the next.

(d) ascending (1) sequence (1). *Note*: remember to describe sequences as ascending or descending.

(e) double (1) appoggiatura (1), one part chromatic (1) resolving to V⁷/dominant 7th (1) in first inversion (1). Max. (3).

(f) bar 51: Ib/tonic in first inversion (1); bar 53: Ia/tonic in root position (1)

(g) three (1)

(h) B (1)

(i) B (1)

2011 Test 4

Based on Edexcel Anthology No. 6 (p. 120), bars 90–132.

(a) B (1)

(b) additive rhythm (1); syncopation (1); (rhythmic) ostinato (1). Max. (2).

(c) heard in transposed version (1) in bass instruments/(first orchestra) cellos and basses (1). Do not credit imitation or antiphony.

(d) (i) augmentation (1)

(ii) the motif is doubled in length/quavers become crotchets (1), then doubled again/with minims (1), finally doubled again/each note taking a whole bar (but with rests for the last beat and a half) (1).

(e) contrapuntal (1), with each part doubled in octaves (1); three parts/with a third part (in the middle, unlike the start of the movement) (1). Max. (2).

(f) pentatonic (1)

(g) E (1); G (1)

(h) B (1)

(i) C (1)

2011 Test 5

Based on Edexcel Anthology No. 55 (p. 496), bars 35–end.

(a) At first/in bars 2–5 all play in <u>octaves</u> (1), with heterophony (1); later/in bars 6–9 reeds and brass play chords/major triads (1) in parallel with bass (1). Max. (2).

(b) syncopation (1); back-beat (1); triplets (1). Max. (2).

(c) same as in bars 2–5 (1); one chord per bar (in bars 6–8) (1), then (much) faster harmonic rhythm/ rate of chord change/more chords in <u>bar 9</u> (1); more varied/adventurous harmony than elsewhere in the piece (1); non-functional (1); chords descending in whole tones (in bar 9) (1); parallel (1) root-position (1) chords. Max. (3).

(d) G♭ (1); D♭ (1); A♭ (1)

(e) stepwise (and/or repeated-note) backing vocals (1); leaps in lead vocals (1) spanning an octave (1); outlining arpeggio/broken chord (1); lead vocals (heavily) syncopated (1), backing vocals begin on the second beat of the bar (1); all text setting syllabic (1) except briefly in lead vocals (1). Max. (3).

(f) homophonic (1)

(g) C (1)

(h) C (1)

2011 Test 6

Based on Edexcel Anthology No. 41 (p. 366), bars 25–46.

(a) vocalising/wordless singing (1) by women's voices (1) in two parts (1) with parallel augmented 4ths/ tritones (1). Max. (2).

(b) two chords (1), moving back and forth (1) in parallel (1) 6ths (1); solo violin (1) – although this is almost inaudible on the anthology CD. Max. (2).

(c) syncopation/push (1)

(d) false relation (1)

(e) pentatonic (1)

(f) portamento (1) up an octave (1) then back down to the original note (1). Max. (2).

(g) chromatic (1)

(h) perfect (1)

(i) sustained chord in upper parts (1), with melody in bass (1) drawing on (vocal) motif previously heard (e.g. at 'goin' to rise') (1), followed by chords leading into next passage (1). Max. (3).

(j)　B (1)

(k)　B (1)

2011 Test 7

Based on Edexcel Anthology No. 11 (p. 171), from 2:30 to 3:15.

(a)　monophonic (1)

(b)　1. snapping fingers (1); 2. mouth click (1); 3. dental tremolo (1); 4. slide (1); 5. mouth closed (1)

(c)　(i) 'u'(1); (ii) 'a' (1); (iii) 'i' (1)

(d)　F♯ (1), D (1), B (1)

(e)　A (1)

(f)　B (1)

(g)　pitches are not always as indicated (1), nor are rhythms (1), and timings need not correspond exactly with the given 10-second divisions given on the score (1). Max. (2).

2011 Test 8

Based on Edexcel Anthology No. 8 (p. 160), bars 16 (on repeat)–43.

(a)　(i) violin (1); (ii) (tenor) sax(ophone) (1); (iii) piano (1); (iv) clarinet (1)

(b)　textures are denser (1); rests are shorter for each instrument (1); ranges are wider (1); louder dynamics/ use of *ff* (1). Max. (2).

(c)　(i) arco (1); (ii) pizz(icato) (1)

(d)　cantus firmus (1) presented in *Klangfarbenmelodie* (1) in violin, clarinet and tenor saxophone (1) with mirror (1) canons (1) on piano (1). Accept 'pointillism' (1). Max. (4).

(e)　(i) augmented 4th/diminished 5th/tritone (1); (ii) minor 7th (1)

(f)　C (1)

(g)　D (1)

Section A: 2012

2012 Test 1

Based on Edexcel Anthology No. 3 (p. 42), bars 166–193.

(a)　(i) (tonic) pedal (1); (ii) lively/dotted/saltarello rhythms (on tonic chord) (1) **or** in diminution/quick §

time (1); (iii) occasional/single pizz(icato) notes (1).

(b)   (solo) viola (1)

(c)   flute (1) and harp (harmonics) (1)

(d)   same melodic shape (1) in ascending (1) sequence (1). Bars 5–7 are (based on a) minor (chord) (1), but bars 2–4 are major (1). Phrase in bars 5–7 begins earlier/a beat ahead in the bar (compared with first phrase) (1). Max. (3).

(e)   minor (1) 6th (1)

(f)   descending (1) sequence (1), with chromaticism in bar 19 (1). Max. (2).

(g)   augmentation (1)

(h)   C (1)

(i)   C (1)

2012 Test 2

Based on Edexcel Anthology No. 37 (p. 359), bars 8–39 (on repeat).

(a)   (melody-dominated) homophony (1)

(b)   suspension (1)

(c)   perfect (1); E major (1). *Note*: instead of E major, you would be given credit for writing 'dominant'.

(d)   chromatic (1)

(e)   (dominant) pedal (1), touching on minor mode (1); heterophonic texture (1), (followed by a) passage in octaves (1), with more rapid rhythms/demisemiquavers (1). Max. (3).

(f)   D major (1)

(g)   IIb (1) but allow IV (*Note*: the correct chord description (IIb) only becomes evident with the sounding of the second semiquaver); Ic (1); V⁷ (1).

(h)   descending (1) (major) scale (1) in 3rds (1). Max (2).

(i)   B (1)

(j)   Any year between 1755 and 1809 (1). The actual date of composition was 1794.

2012 Test 3

Based on Edexcel Anthology No. 15 (p. 200), bars 20–43.

(a)   violin(s) (1); cello (1); (chamber) organ (1)

(b)   imitation (1) at unison (1) after one bar (1), then at the 5th/12th below (1). Accept 'contrapuntal' (1). Max. (2).

(c) hemiola (1)

(d) (i) B minor (1); (ii) E minor (1)

(e) interrupted (1)

(f) (C) natural (1)

(g) suspension (1)

(h) D major (1); perfect (1)

(i) (trio) sonata (1)

(j) A (1)

(k) B (1)

2012 Test 4

Based on Edexcel Anthology No. 31 (p. 307), bars 7–26.

(a) (double) octaves (1). (*Note*: in an analytical context, 'unison' is too inexact, even though when men and women sing the same tune in octaves (as sometimes in church services) this is informally referred to as 'unison'.)

(b) <u>minor</u> 3rd (1)

(c) cello(s) (1); (double) bass(es) (1)

(d) tenor(s) (1); bass(es) (1); octave (1)

(e) A (1)

(f) ostinato (1)

(g) augmented 4th/tritone (1). Accept instead 'diminished 5th'.

(h) <u>major</u> 3rd(s)/chord (1) without 5th (1), but with minor/dominant 7th (above bass/root) (1). Max (2).

(i) bassoon(s) (1); horn(s) (1)

(j) (double) bass(es) (1); pizzicato (1). In an exam, you *may* get the second mark for writing 'plucked', but it is wiser to use the standard term 'pizzicato'.

2012 Test 5

Based on Edexcel Anthology No. 17 (p. 207), bars 111–164.

(a) C (1)

(b) (i) clarinet (1); (ii) horn (1); (iii) violin (1)

(c) (i) A♭ major (1); (ii) F minor (1)

(d)   staccato/detached (1) crotchets (1) grouped in threes (1) in octaves (1). Max. (2).

(e)   dominant (1) pedal (1). (*Note*: in a two-mark question about pedals, one mark will be awarded for 'pedal'. The other mark will be for additional information, commonly the scale degree used (normally 'tonic' or 'dominant'), or for noting where a pedal is 'inverted' (used not in the bass but in the highest part).)

(f)   dominant 7th/V^z (1)

(g)   chromatic (1)

(h)   turn (1)

(i)   perfect (1)

(j)   B (1)

(k)   C (1)

2012 Test 6

Based on Edexcel Anthology No. 54 (p. 487), bars 58–78.

(a)   homophonic (1), with piano chords/comping (1); bass guitar playing an ornamented/heterophonic version of bass (1); orchestral parts in octaves (1). Max. (2).

(b)   (part of) (reverse) circle of 5ths/chords rising in 5ths/falling in 4ths (1)

(c)   (prominent) stepwise (1) bass in orchestra on brass instruments (1) under parallel (1) root position chords (1) all major/E, D and C (1). Max. (2).

(d)   (rhythm) guitar added (1); no orchestra (1)

(e)   (descending) perfect 4th (1); (ascending) perfect 5th (1). Award (1) mark instead just for rising as opposed to falling.

(f)
 B (1) C (1) [B] A (1)

They   had   to   count_   them all!__

(g)   In bars 18–19, (pairs of) semiquavers (each) fall a semitone (1), while in bars 19–21 they rise a semitone (1); in bars 18–19, the overall shape of phrase is ascending (1), whereas in bars 19–21 it is descending (1); in bars 18–19, word-setting is syllabic (1), whereas in bars 19–21 it is melismatic (1). Max. (3).

(h)   C (1)

2012 Test 7

Based on Edexcel Anthology No. 34 (p. 349), bars 1–43.

(a)   imitation (at the unison) (1)

(b)   (perfect) 5th (1)

(c)   hemiola (1)

(d)   D (major) (1)

(e)   canon/imitation (1) at the unison (1) at one beat's distance/one beat behind (1). Max. (2).

(f)   homophonic/chordal/homorhythmic (1)

(g)   dialogue (1) between two (1) pairs of parts (1) at the same pitch (1), while the other/middle/fifth part has a narrowly moving (1) cantus-firmus-like part (1). Accept instead reference to imitation (1) at the unison (1). Max (4).

(h)   (G major) IV/C major chord (1); (G major) V/D major chord (1); (G major) I/G major chord (1)

(i)   ballett (1). Accept instead madrigal.

(j)   A (1)

2012 Test 8

Based on Edexcel Anthology No. 31 (p. 307), bars 150–168.

(a)   soprano(s) (1); bass(es) (1)

(b)   canon/imitation/pedal/ostinato (in bass) (1)

(c)   (first) oboe(s) (1)

(d)   melody plus <u>contrapuntal</u> accompaniment (1); <u>soprano</u>/<u>melody</u> **either** (rises) alternately (1) in semitones and tones (1) **or** uses an octatonic scale (2), above imitation (1) based on theme from bar 1/using dotted rhythms (1). Max. (3).

(e)   homophonic/chordal (1)

(f)   slower (1)

(g)   sopranos move narrowly/have a range of a (minor) 3rd (1) with semitonal/chromatic movement near end (C–Db–D♮ etc.) (1); altos and/or tenors/inner part(s) have very narrow ranges (also) (1); bass has repeated octave leaps (falling and rising from Bb to Bb) (1); bass doubles soprano (at the octave) <u>near end</u> (1); mostly syllabic/(occasional) short melismas (1). Max. (3).

(h)   (even) minims (1); ostinato (1) of <u>four</u> notes (1) within the <u>triple</u>/$\frac{3}{2}$ time signature (1) based on (falling and rising) (perfect) 4ths (1)/Eb–Bb–F–Bb (1). Max. (3).

(i)

(1)

2013 Test 1

Based on Edexcel Anthology No. 5 (p. 86), bars 75–90.

(a)   (i) clarinet (1); (ii) violin (1); (iii) flute (1)

(b)   first inversion (1) chord (1) sustained (1) by strings (1), with broken chords (1) in harp (1). Max. (3).

(c)   variation of preceding flute theme/Faun's theme (1) in shorter note values (accept diminution) (1), with narrower range/minor 3rd (1), (entirely) chromatic writing (1), and ornamentation/trill (1). Max. (3).

(d)   (almost exact) repetition (1)

(e)   descending figure passed between various wind sections (1) in this order: flute(s) to oboe(s) (and cor anglais) (1), clarinet(s) with bassoon(s) (1), horn(s) (1). Max. (2).

(f)   same harmony and melody (1), now a semitone lower/in E♭ (1), the melody on oboe (1). Max. (2).

(g)   B (1)

(h)   C (1)

2013 Test 2

Based on Edexcel Anthology No. 35 (p. 353), bars 1–29.

(a)   homophony (1) in three parts (1)

(b)   higher (1) by a 3rd/in B♭ (major) (1) instead of G minor (1); with a (stronger) tritonal/augmented 4th (1) dissonance between the outer parts (1). Max. (3).

(c)   imperfect (1)

(d)   a 3rd (1) higher (1), with a diminished 5th (instead of a perfect 5th) (1); sung by a different part (canto not quinto) (1). Max. (2).

(e)   B (1). *Note*: three parts of this question – (b), (d) and (e) – require you to recognise the important interval of a 3rd. 'Real' exam questions are unlikely to be so insistent on a single point – but we have been so here, to emphasise the importance of being able to recognise 3rds, which are important in so many types of music.

(f)   D minor (1); perfect (1); tierce de Picardie (1)

(g)   homophonic/homorhythmic/chordal (1); three parts (1)

(h)   bar 8 (1)

(i)   B (1)

2013 Test 3

Based on Edexcel Anthology No. 19 (p. 242), bars 1–25.

(a)   trumpet (in C) (1)

(b)   G (major) (1); perfect (1)

(c)   in bars 5–6: trumpet rhythm changed/no semiquavers (1); horn's quaver patterns different (some reversed) (1); horn's C♯ was originally C♮ (1); trombone has <u>minims/minim</u> Gs (1) (instead of crotchet Gs in bars 1–2); there is a (fourth) minim G (instead of the C in bar 2) (1), with (chord IV in G being changed to) V⁷(d) in D (1). Max. (4).

(d)   D (major) (1)

(e)   faster (1)

(f)   octave (1) lower (1); louder (1); more staccato notes (1); ends differently (1) without semiquavers (1). Max. (3).

(g)   fragmented/shared between (the three) instruments (1); descending triad shape (1) heard in various rhythms/with augmentation in trombone (1) first major <u>then minor</u> (1). Max. (2).

(h)   D (1)

(i)   C (1)

2013 Test 4

Based on Edexcel Anthology No. 51 (p. 471), bars 37–26 (repeat).

(a)   vocalisation/melismatic (1)

(b)   <u>lead</u> guitar (1)

(c)

(d)   harmonica (1)

(e)   slide (1); chords/triple stopping (1)

(f)   vocal has melody (1); instruments accompany (1), with chords on strong beats (of bars 15–17) (1) and fills (1) in lead guitar and/or drums (1). Max. (3).

(g)   C⁹ (1) but accept C⁷; G⁷ (1); D⁷ (1)

(h)   swung/shuffle (1)

(i)   B (1)

(j)   C (1)

2013 Test 5

Based on Edexcel Anthology No. 12 (p. 176), bars 21–53.

(a)   all woodwind/all from one woodwind family/type (1); (eight/nine) clarinets (eight are pre-recorded, one is played live) (1) and (two) bass clarinets (1)

(b)   **either** descending (1) by step (1) to (major) triad(ic shape)/B–G♯–E (1) **or** arpeggiated (1) added-6th chord (1). Max. (2).

(c)   (built largely on) major chords (1) of V/F♯ major (1) and IV/E major (1). These alternate and overlap (1) giving a static (1) non-cadential/non-functional (1) effect. Max. (3).

(d)   dissonant/added-note chords (1) (added) underneath (1), (rapidly) repeated (1), each for several bars at a time (1). Max. (2).

(e)   counterpoint in upper parts (1), involving close (1) imitation/canon (1); joined by lowest instruments in pulsing/rapidly repeated (1) homophony (1). Max. (4).

(f)   C (1)

(g)   C (1)

2013 Test 6

Based on Edexcel Anthology No. 32 (p. 344), bars 1–7.

(a)   bar 1 is monophonic (1); bar 2 is two-part (1) and homorhythmic/homophonic/counterpoint of two rhythmically identical melodies (1)

(b)   G (major) (1)

(c)   B (1)

(d)   exactly the same (1) (apart from different words)

(e)   retrograde/backwards (1)

(f)   third/sixth (quavers: F♮ and A) (1)

(g)   'bright' (1)

(h)   homophonic/homorhythmic/chordal (1) in four parts (1)

(i)   suspension/9–8 (suspension) (1); perfect (1); E modal (1) minor (1)

(j)   A (1)

2013 Test 7

Based on Edexcel Anthology No. 22 (p. 253), bars 1–31.

(a)

(1)

(Appoggiatura. Allow quaver appoggiatura (♪), but not acciaccatura.)

(b)   melody (1) plus (quaver) broken-chord accompaniment (1)/melody-dominated homophony (1); two parts (1). Max. (2).

(c)   syncopation (1)

(d)   IIb (1), V/Ic–V (1) and I (1)/perfect cadence (2); double (1) suspension (at bar 9, beat 3) (1), 9–8 and/ or 7–6 (1). Accept, instead of a reference to Ic, double appoggiatura at bar 9 beat 4 (1). No dissonance in bar 10 (1). Max. (4).

(e)   accented passing note (1). Such a prominent dissonance can alternatively (and correctly) be described as an appoggiatura, even though it is not approached by a leap.

(f)   imperfect (1); F (major) (1). *Note*: the cadence ends with a C major chord after a passage containing some B♮s. However this is not the key of C major (unlikely in a Classical-period piece that begins in B♭ major) but F major, in readiness for the second subject at bar 23, with some *chromatic* B♮s.

(g)   homophonic (1)

(h)   (harmonic) sequence (1)

(i)   bar 31: the chord at beat 1 has fewer parts/is less dense (1); extra bass note on beat 2 (1). Max. (1).

(j)   B (1)

(k)   B (1)

2013 Test 8

Based on Edexcel Anthology No. 56 (p. 501), bars 21–36.

(a)   sax(ophone) (1)

(b)   three-part (1) counterpoint/contrapuntal (1), which is free/non-imitative (1) except that acoustic guitar echoes sax <u>at beginning</u> (1), (above) bass, which outlines the harmonies (1); electric guitar is generally the highest (1) and most melodic part (1); piano provides chords/comping (1). Max. (4).

(c)

(1) (1)(1)

(Accept instead notes written an octave lower)

(d)   syncopation (1); alternates (1) between two notes/F and D (1); electric guitar melody (in) <u>very</u> high (register) (1). Max. (2).

(e)   electric guitar <u>begins with</u> (four) quavers (1) but has (mainly) (groups of four) semiquavers (1); acoustic guitar has (mainly) triplet (quavers) (1). Max. (2).

(f)   Dm (1); E♭ (1); B♭ (1)

(g)   B (1)

2013 Test 9

Based on Edexcel Anthology No. 19 (p. 242), bars 34–56.

(a)   (even/all) crotchets (1)

(b)   (at first) leaps (up and down) two octaves (1), getting louder/*f*, *ff*, *fff* (1), then (long/big) scalic (1) descent (1) (mostly) in semiquavers (1), with some chromatic movement/E♮–E♭ (1). Max. (3).

(c)   B♭ (major) (1); V/V⁷ (1)

(d)   homophonic (1); (all notes) staccato (1); trombone and trumpet alternate (1) together with a (more-or-less) continuous part for horn (1) making a two-part texture (1). Max. (3).

(e) perfect (1); F (major) (1)

(f) second phrase: ends with a scalic run (down) (1) from C (1); articulation different (1). Max. (2).

(g) trumpet run different (1) – C Db Eb F Gb/(mostly) a semitone lower (1); dynamics and/or articulation different (1); repeated chords different (1) implying different 7th chords (1). Max. (2).

(h) B (1)

2013 Test 10

Based on Edexcel Anthology No. 35 (p. 353), bars 39–67.

(a) same rhythm (1); a 3rd (1) lower (1) except <u>at one point</u> where it is a 4th lower (1). Max. (2).

(b) G minor (1)

(c) <u>begins</u> with repeated chords (of Bb major) (1); parallel (1) $\frac{6}{3}$/first-inversion triads (1), with false relations (1); two-chord (1) sequential (1) pattern. Max. (4).

(d) (tonic) pedal (1)

(e) five-part (1) homophonic/homorhythmic/chordal (1)

(f) three (1)

(g) chords IIIb (1) to I (1)/a variant/distorted perfect cadence (1). Tierce de Picardie in final chord (1). Max. (2).

(h) repetition of 'Ohimè' arising from 'thousands' in the text (1); minor mode (1); dissonances (portray the singers' mock agony) (1); if not previously mentioned, false relations (1). Max. (2).

(i) C (1)

2013 Test 11

Based on Edexcel Anthology No. 56 (p. 501), bars 1–20.

(a) flute (1)

(b) B (1)

(c) lead vocal has melody (1); instruments accompany (1), although bass has melodic qualities as well (1); electric guitar fill(s) (1) partly double the bass (1); piano has comping (1); regular on-the-beat drum part (1). Max. (4).

(d) Eb (1); F (1); Bb (1)

(e) one phrase (1) not two (1); ends/is mostly higher (1); includes a triplet (1); phrase in bar 16 finishes on dominant (1), bar 14 on tonic (1); bar 15 has (the largest melodic interval) – a (falling) perfect 4th (1). Max. (3).

(f)

(g)   B♭ (major) (1); plagal (1)

(h)   C (1)

Test paper for 2011

Section A: Question 1

Based on Edexcel Anthology No. 21 (p. 249), Gigue, bars 49–96 (second time).

(a)   (i) one (1); (ii) two (1); (iii) three (1)

(b)   descending (1) sequence (1)

(c)   (i) B minor (1); (ii) E minor (1)

(d)   (part of a) circle of fifths (1). Accept instead 'sequence'.

(e)   two C naturals, (1) for lower and (1) for upper

(f)   (i) tonic/I/D (major) (1); (ii) diminished 7th/G♯ B D F (inverted) (1)

(g)   perfect (1)

(h)   A (1)

(i)   B (1)

(j)   C (1)

Section A: Question 2

Based on Edexcel Anthology No. 33 (p. 347), bars 9–24.

(a)   lute (1); (bass) viol (1)

(b)   C major (1)

(c)   (i) dialogue/antiphonal exchange (1), parallel 6ths/10ths (1); (ii) imitation (1) in three parts (1). Max. (3).

(d)   Phrygian/imperfect/half-close (1)

(e)   They ascend/are inverted (1) and include a G♯/span a diminished 4th (1)/G♯–A–B–C instead of C–B–A–G♮ (2).

(f)   perfect 4th (1); sequence (1)

(g)   A minor (1); perfect (1); suspension *or* tierce de Picardie (1)

(h)   ayre/lute song (1)

(i)   C (1)

Section B Indicative Content

For each Section B question, it is impossible to give a totally comprehensive mark scheme that lists all the possible points you might make. Instead, we provide for each question what examiners term 'indicative content' – that is, a list of the main relevant points

For detailed guidance on how to implement mark schemes, ask your teacher and/or see the Sample Assessment Materials, pages 71, 78 and 80. (The SAMs may be accessed from the Edexcel website.) Mark schemes from past examinations are also available.

3 (a) (i) Tippett

➢ Rhythmically independent parts reflect interest in English Renaissance music, notably madrigals
➢ Other Renaissance techniques evident in use of antiphony and counterpoint, including imitation by inversion
➢ Modality, as opposed to functional tonality
➢ Final open 5th chord also a Renaissance feature. Phrygian cadence (bars 20–21) common in Renaissance and Baroque periods
➢ Compare Baroque structural approach with use of 'ritornello'
➢ Melodic sequence is also a feature of Baroque melody writing
➢ Opposition of two balanced forces (compare Baroque concertato style)
➢ Reliance on Classical structural schemes, i.e. sonata form with contrasting keys.

Credit up to three clear examples as additional points.

3 (a) (ii) Haydn and Webern

1. Texture

Haydn

Melody-dominated homophony, with melody almost entirely in first violin; texture varies between three- and four-part; frequent use of pedals, both sustained and reiterated notes; some dialogue/'imitation' between first violin, second violin and viola in 3rds, and cello; homophony in Adagio, with some five- and six-note chords through double-stopping; use of complete silent bars/G.P.

Webern

Mainly contrapuntal with two-part/mirror canons; texture very sparse, only occasionally with more than two notes sounding simultaneously/'pointilliste' [i.e. 'dots' of sound, with very wide use of rests within each part]; prime [the original form of the tone row] announced by sax as a sort of 'cantus firmus'; later presented in *Klangfarbenmelodie*; climax results from increasing density of texture, with more instruments playing simultaneously.

2. Use of instruments

Haydn

All four instruments from same family; conventional playing techniques (bowed throughout), with isolated examples of double stopping; instrumental ranges fairly narrow by some later standards; some relatively limited exploitation of *sf* and *f–p* contrasts.

Webern

Mixed ensemble, with wide range of timbres; rapidly alternating performance techniques (pizz./arco; mutes on and off); extreme ranges; extreme dynamics.

Credit up to six clear examples as additional points.

3 (b) (i) Bruckner

➢ Relatively wide range in melody line (compared with church music from previous eras/Renaissance church music)
➢ Some typically Romantic wider intervals, for example 7ths and octaves
➢ Chromaticism
➢ Functional harmony, including sevenths, sometimes inverted
➢ Romantic-era chord choice embraces diminished sevenths
➢ Unprepared dissonance
➢ 'Cecilian' work within Romantic tradition, deliberately cultivating simpler styles that are in part indebted to Renaissance music (e.g. *a cappella* writing), with more traditional features such as suspensions and Phrygian cadences
➢ Some tonal ambiguity arising from chromaticism
➢ The relatively wide range of texture is common in Romantic era, e.g. homophony and imitation by inversion.

Credit up to three clear examples as additional points.

3 (b) (ii) Gershwin and You can get it

1. Word-setting

Gershwin

Mainly syllabic, with occasional two-note slurs; some portamento; no textual repetitions.

You can get it

Mainly syllabic except for three- or four-note melismas at ends of phrases; frequent textual repetition.

2. Melody

Gershwin

Almost completely pentatonic minor (i.e. B, D, E, F♯ and A), except for C♯; spans an octave, with mainly small intervals; four-bar phrases, four to a verse.

You can get it

Largely pentatonic major; narrow range at first, with phrases spanning a 3rd and frequent repetitions; wider range at end of verse and in coda, melody going higher, rising in 3rds.

3. Rhythm

Gershwin

Lullaby effect achieved through steadily rocking chords; in (simple) duple time; with swung/dotted rhythm; a few triplets (in orchestral 'fills'); syncopation (leans and pushes); numerous long notes in solo vocal part (during which other parts are more active); continuous quavers in solo violin (against the minims of the backing vocals).

You can get it

Vocal parts start on second beat in quadruple time ; frequent quavers, with syncopation and some (crotchet) triplets; longer notes in contrasting instrumental motif (bars 36–43).

Credit up to six clear examples as additional points.

Section C: Question 4

Source: 'The Farmer's Boy' (English traditional), verse 1 and chorus. Specially arranged for this volume.

(a)   (B♭ major) Ib (1); IV (1)

(b)   auxiliary note (1)

(c)   dominant 7th/V⁷ (1)

(d)   F major (1). Accept instead 'dominant'.

(e)   diminished 7th (1)

(f)   D (1)

(g)   (dominant) pedal (1)

Section C: Question 5

Note: marking harmony exercises is far from straightforward – ask your teacher to help you with the marking of this test.

We haven't given a correct answer, because there will be several possible correct answers to harmony exercises. The music for Question 5 has been specially composed.

For Question 5, 12 marks are available.

For choosing appropriate chords and for correct part-writing: 10 marks are available.

Give two marks for each chord that has been chosen appropriately and is correct in terms of part-writing (that is, without consecutive 5ths and other such faults).

Give one mark where:

➢   A chord is an unsuitable choice, but is not totally wrong.
  For example, imagine that someone wrote, in C major, chords III–I at the end of a phrase, under the notes B and C. The chord III would be unsuitable, because there's no such cadence as III–I. But if the part-writing connected with the III–I progression were correct, 1 mark could still be awarded for the chord III (and 2 marks for the chord I).
➢   A chord contains one obviously wrong note (e.g. in C–E–F–C the F makes no sense – the writer clearly meant, but did not succeed in writing, a C major chord with C–E–G–C).
➢   A chord has one note missing.
➢   A chord has one part-writing problem, which probably means that this chord:
  ➢   Marks the end of a single set of consecutive 5ths or octaves
  ➢   Has a doubling of the leading note
  ➢   Has some other problem with doubling (e.g. a root-position chord has no 3rd – C–C–G–C with no E)
  ➢   Has unsuitable spacing (notably with more than an octave between neighbouring upper parts)
  ➢   Has parts that cross for no good reason
  ➢   Has parts that overlap for no good reason
  ➢   Stands at the end of an unsuitable melodic interval (probably an augmented 2nd or 4th).

Give no mark where a chord:

➢   Is unsuitable *and* there is one part-writing problem
➢   Has two part-writing problems
➢   Has two obviously wrong notes

➤ Has two notes missing.

For special features: 2 marks are available

Give one mark for each special feature correctly used.

'Special features' are mainly appropriate non-harmonic notes (sometimes referred to as 'non-chord' notes, or as 'unessential notes') such as passing notes and suspensions, but also include a final tierce de Picardie in a perfect cadence in a minor key.

Test paper for 2012

Section A: Question 1

Based on Edexcel Anthology No. 23 (p. 258), no. 11, bars 13–48.

(a) (i) G major (1) imperfect (1); (ii) E minor (1) interrupted (1); (iii) B minor (with tierce de Picardie)/ accept B major (1) perfect (1)

(b) (melody-dominated) homophony (1) with left hand (sometimes) in 6ths with right hand/parallel 6ths (1), then left hand has alternating low single notes (1) and (off-beat) chords (1). Max. (2).

(c) (left-hand and right-hand) parts exchanged (1); triads in right hand (1) instead of 3rds in left hand (1); (almost entirely) diatonic (1); perfect cadence (1) instead of imperfect (1). Max. (3).

(d) sudden changes of tempo (1), strong dynamic contrast (especially $\it{ff}$ in bar 9) (1), off-beat stresses (1), chromaticism (1), unstable key (1). Max. (3).

(e) C (1)

(f) A (1)

Section A: Question 2

Based on Edexcel Anthology No. 52 (p. 477), bars 74–end.

(a) (double/upright/string) bass (1) (bass guitar = 0)

(b) (i) lead guitar (1); (ii) (perfect) 4th (1); (iii) E (major) (1); (iv) C (major) (1)

(c) same pitches, different rhythm/heterophony (1). *Note*: here heterophony only involves rhythmic differences between the parts.

(d) swung/dotted (1) syncopated (1)

(e) mostly monotone/on a single note (1) E (1), with occasional blue notes (1) (approximating to) D natural (1), G natural (1), and one unpitched note (1); short phrases (1) with verbal repetition (1) and scat singing (1). Max. (3).

(f) (i) A (major) (1); (ii) B^7 (1); (iii) E (major) (with added) <u>6</u>(th) (1)

(g) B (1)

(h) D (1)

Section B Indicative Content

For each Section B question, it is impossible to give a totally comprehensive mark scheme that lists all the possible points you might make. Instead, we provide for each question what examiners term 'indicative content' – that is, a list of the main relevant areas of information.

For detailed guidance on how to implement mark schemes, ask your teacher and/or see the Sample Assessment Materials, pages 71, 78 and 80. (The SAMs may be accessed from the Edexcel website.) Mark schemes from past examinations are also available.

3 (a) (i) Corelli

➤ Baroque trio sonata for two high melody instruments of similar range and bass continuo, with the harmony realised on organ
➤ Polarised texture, with some counterpoint, imitation, stretto, pedal points
➤ Resembles/based on gigue – a standard stylised dance in the Baroque era
➤ Hemiola
➤ Harmony indicated by figured bass, including suspensions, circle of fifths
➤ Tonality evident in functional harmonic progressions and cadences, as well as modulations to nearly-related keys.

Credit up to three clear examples as additional points.

3 (a) (ii) Berlioz and Beethoven

1. Melody

Berlioz

Based mainly on three distinct melodies; the first in saltarello style is conjunct, revolves around E, and consists of one-bar cells which together form longer irregular phrases; some modal inflections; the second 'serenade' theme starts with broken chord pattern, and again has phrases irregular in length; the third is the *idée fixe*; some sequence and repetition (in all three melodies).

Beethoven

Introduction contains mixture of broken-chord, conjunct movement and repeated notes (with acciccaturas); first subject outlines rising broken chord; some chromaticism; ornamental turn (at cadence); appoggiaturas; balanced (periodic) phrasing frequent.

2. Harmony

Berlioz

Largely functional progressions, with seventh chords, occasional diminished sevenths, pedals/drones, relatively slow harmonic rhythm.

Beethoven

Functional progressions with clearly defined (perfect and imperfect) cadences; some chromatic chords, e.g. augmented 6th; harmonic rhythm speeds up to cadences.

Credit up to six clear examples as additional points.

3 (b) (i) Haydn

➤ Domestic song (of a type cultivated in late 18th-century England) with piano accompaniment, which mostly doubles vocal part
➤ Accompaniment fully notated, not Baroque-style continuo part

> Strophic with introduction which announces main theme
> Melody-dominated homophony, with occasional heterophony (between piano right hand and voice)
> Balanced/periodic phrasing
> Broken-chord melody followed by conjunct lines; appoggiaturas; occasional chromaticism
> Classical-style functional harmony (with much emphasis on I and V⁷); clearly defined cadences and modulation to dominant.

Credit up to three clear examples as additional points.

3 (b) (ii) Weelkes and the Beatles

1. Structure

Weelkes

Two main sections, repeated (with voice exchange in second section); each section ending with a fa la refrain.

The Beatles

Combination of two songs; introduction followed by three verses of different lengths; transitional section; second song as bridge/contrasting section; a second transition leading to return of first song for a final verse; coda.

2. Tonality

Weelkes

Mixolydian mode – broadly equivalent to G major with clear cadences, and brief references to closely related/dominant and subdominant keys; some (interval/inverted) pedal notes.

The Beatles

Modal elements; moves from G to E in bridge; reverse circle of 5ths; returns to G, then closes in E.

Credit up to six clear examples as additional points.

Section C: Question 4

Source: 'Die Alte' ('The Old Woman'), K.517, by Mozart (verse 1). An 18th-century old woman (like one or two of her 21st-century counterparts?) is complaining about standards of life and behaviour compared to those 'in my time' – 'zu meiner Zeit'.

(a)   (E minor) V (1); Ib (1); V⁷b (1)

(b)   B minor (1); A minor (1)

(c)   perfect (1)

(d)   anticipation (1)

(e)   A (1)

Section C: Question 5

See test paper for 2011, Question 5 (pages 83–84).

Test paper for 2013

Section A: Question 1

Based on Edexcel Anthology No. 22 (p. 253), bars 63⁴–97.

(a)   descending sequence (1)

(b)   diminished 7th (1); second (1); V (1); perfect (1)

(c)   F minor (1)

(d)   melody (1) plus Alberti bass (1)/(melody-dominated) homophony (1); two-part (1). Max. (2).

(e)   syncopation (1)

(f)   G minor (1); imperfect (1)

(g)   less frequently (1). Note: the prolonged dominant harmony (chord V, V⁷ and V with a flattened 9th) helps prepare the listener for the approach of the recapitulation, with the return of the probably well-remembered opening theme. Prolonged use of chord V is a favourite Classical way of saying to the listener: 'Wait for it… something very important is about to happen!'

(h)   B♭ major (1); appoggiatura (1); (upward-resolving) suspension and appoggiatura (1), but accept instead double suspension/double appoggiatura

(i)   C (1)

Section A: Question 2

Based on Edexcel Anthology No. 33 (p. 347), bars 9–24.

(a)   lute (1); (bass) viol (1)

(b)   C major (1)

(c)   (i) dialogue/antiphonal exchange (1), parallel 6ths/10ths (1); (ii) imitation (1) in three parts (1). Max. (3).

(d)   Phrygian/imperfect/half-close (1)

(e)   They ascend/are inverted (1) and include a G♯/span a _diminished_ 4th (1)/G♯–A–B–C instead of C–B–A–G♮ (2).

(f)   perfect 4th (1); sequence (1)

(g)   A minor (1); perfect (1); suspension _or_ tierce de Picardie (1)

(h)   ayre/lute song (1)

(i)   C (1)

Section B Indicative Content

For each Section B question, it is impossible to give a totally comprehensive mark scheme that lists all the possible points you might make. Instead, we provide for each question what examiners term 'indicative content' – that is, a list of the main relevant areas of information.

For detailed guidance on how to implement mark schemes, ask your teacher and/or see the Sample Assessment Materials, pages 71, 78 and 80. (The SAMs may be accessed from the Edexcel website.) Mark schemes from past examinations are also available.

3 (a) (i) Debussy

➢ Flexible rhythm and metre, with numerous triplet and sextuplet groupings
➢ Melodies embracing chromaticism, tritones, whole-tone elements
➢ Non-functional harmony, with unresolved dissonance; 7th, 9th, 11th, and 13th chords. Few clear cadences, and sometimes ambiguous tonality. Fluid modulation to wide range of keys
➢ New sensitivity to timbre and orchestral colour, with numerous special effects, e.g. tremolandi.

Credit up to three clear examples as additional points.

3 (a) (ii) Reich and Poulenc

1. Texture

Reich

Phasing/contrapuntal with close imitation/canon; pulsing/rapidly repeating four-part homophony/chords fading in and out under counterpoint in central part of piece.

Poulenc

Melody-dominated homophony, with melody in various parts of texture; occasional monophony; octaves; various accompanying figurations.

2. Tonality

Reich

Entirely diatonic, though non-functional, with absence of cadence/drive to tonic because of repetition of IV and V in B major.

Poulenc

Underlying functional schemes adorned with wrong-note harmony, e.g. cadences; clearly defined tonal centres with switches of key to dominant, then to tertiary related keys; dominant preparation; some ambiguity, for example in closing section because of chromaticism.

Credit up to six clear examples as additional points.

3 (b) (i) Monteverdi

➢ Seconda prat(t)ica approach: the text is master of the music
➢ Considerable variation of rhythm to reflect speech rhythm and for dramatic effect
➢ Melodic shapes also reflect cadences of speech (notably falling 3rd on 'Ohimè'); some chromaticism; unexpected intervals
➢ Dissonances not always prepared or resolved conventionally
➢ Modal elements persist
➢ Freely varied textures to reflect meaning of text
➢ Homophony used frequently to ensure audibility of words
➢ Through-composed, with frequent breaks between sections; unified, however, by falling 3rd.

Credit up to three clear examples as additional points.

3 (b) (ii) Tavener and Tupelo Honey

1. Word-setting

Tavener

Generally syllabic; occasional (melismatic) slurring of two notes, often to emphasise important syllables.

Tupelo

(Mainly) syllabic, with occasional (melismatic) slurrings of two or three notes.

2. Metre

Tavener

No time signature; bars of varying lengths; consists chiefly of successions of equal notes, but mainly follows speech rhythm

Tupelo

Notated in common time, but to be performed freely throughout.

3. Rhythm

Tavener

Even quavers at starts of phrases, ending with longer notes (crotchets or dotted crotchets); final phrase of each verse rhythmically augmented.

Tupelo

Complex rhythmic notation, involving syncopation, cross-rhythms, various groupings, e.g. triplets, demisemiquavers.

Credit up to six clear examples as additional points.

Section C: Question 4

Source: music specially composed; words anon.

(a)   imperfect (1)

(b)   (E♭ major) VI (1); Vb (1); V⁷ (1)

(c)   (unaccented) passing note (1)

(d)   C minor (1)

(e)   (E♭ major) II⁷b (1)

(f)   plagal (1)

Section C: Question 5

See test paper for 2011, Question 5 (pages 83–84).

Glossary

This glossary is not comprehensive: it refers to terms as used in this volume. For more information about harmonic terms (e.g. suspension), see the AS Harmony Workbook *and/or the* A2 Harmony Workbook *by Hugh Benham (Rhinegold, 2008). For fuller definitions of other terms and expressions, consult the* Dictionary of Music in Sound *by David Bowman (Rhinegold, 2002).*

A cappella. *A cappella* singing is for voices alone, unaccompanied by instruments

Acciaccatura. A very short ornamental note played before a principal melodic note, written or printed as ♪.

Added-note chord. Most chords, in root position, have two or more 3rds above the root in the bass. Generally, an added-note chord includes a 2nd or 6th above the root in the bass; this 2nd or 6th forms part of the harmony and is not a non-harmony (i.e. non-chord) note.

Additive rhythm. Where a bar has beats of unequal lengths, or simply where unequal short rhythmic sets are grouped together to form a longer rhythmic pattern.

Aeolian mode. A scale that uses the following pattern of tones (T) and semitones (s): T–s–T–T–s–T–T. When starting on A, it consists of all the white notes within one octave on a keyboard.

Alberti bass. A particular type of broken-chord pattern often found in Classical keyboard music with three pitches heard in the order low–high–middle–high (e.g. C–G–E–G).

Aleatoric. Music that has elements created or governed by chance, such as the rolling of dice to generate rhythm for a melody or to choose the order of melodic fragments. From the Latin *alea*, meaning a die.

Anthem. A type of church music for choir, often accompanied by organ, and occasionally by larger forces. An anthem usually has English words (often from the Bible).

Anticipation. A melody note (frequently the tonic of the key in the highest part) sounded slightly before the chord to which it belongs, thereby creating a dissonance with the previous chord.

Antiphony. Performance by different singers/instrumentalists in alternation. Often – but not always – the different groups perform similar material.

Appoggiatura. A non-chord note that sounds on the beat as a dissonance and then resolves by step (up or down) to the main chord note. The dissonant note is not 'prepared' as a suspension is. Although appoggiaturas are normally approached by leap, accented passing notes that are particularly long and/or prominent are often described as appoggiaturas, even though they are approached by step. Sometimes an appoggiatura, especially in the Classical period, is indicated by a note in small type, followed by its resolution printed at normal size.

Arco. A direction to bow notes on a string instrument.

Articulation. Articulation concerns the degree to which notes, small groups of notes, or even whole phrases, are separated from those around them. For example, in a legato performance the progression from one note to the next is as smooth as possible, while staccato notes are clearly detached.

Atonal. Atonal music avoids keys or modes; that is, no pitch stands out consistently in the way that the tonic does in tonal music.

Augmentation. The lengthening of the rhythmic values of a previously-heard melody (e.g. where ♩♪♪ has become ♩♩♩).

Augmented 4th. The interval of a 4th which is one semitone larger than a perfect 4th. Like the diminished 5th (which consists of the same number of semitones), it is sometimes described as a **tritone**.

Augmented-6th chord. A chromatic chord which in root position spans the interval of an augmented 6th, e.g. A♭–F♯. The chord also includes the major 3rd above the root (and sometimes also the perfect 5th or augmented 4th).

Auxiliary note. A non-chord note that occurs between, and is a tone or semitone above or below, two harmony notes of the same pitch.

Avant-garde. (French for 'vanguard'.) A label applied to composers or compositions considered to depart radically from previously accepted styles of composition.

Ballett. A lighter type of madrigal (a form of secular vocal music cultivated in Italy and England in the 16th and early 17th centuries), with fa-la-la refrains and a generally syllabic setting.

Bebop. A style of jazz that developed in the 1940s from swing. More complex and less easy to dance to, it was characterised by improvisation, fast tempos, irregular phrase lengths and a greater emphasis on the rhythm section.

Binary form. A type of musical structure with two balancing sections, each usually repeated. The first generally ends in a key other than the tonic; the second ends in the tonic.

Bitonal. Bitonal music uses two different keys simultaneously.

Blue note. A note (usually the 3rd, 5th or 7th degree of a major scale) performed at a slightly lower pitch than normal for expressive effect.

Bridge. In jazz and pop music, a short, contrasting passage that connects two longer sections.

Bridge passage. In a sonata-form movement, the passage between the first and second subjects; it is generally used in the Exposition to effect the modulation from the tonic key of the first subject to the different key of the second subject.

Britpop. A type of rock music that developed in Britain during the 1990s. Strongly influenced by British guitar pop music from the 1960s and 1970s, important Britpop bands include Oasis and Blur.

Cadence. A pair of chords signifying the end of a phrase in tonal music. Cadences are of several types, of which perfect and imperfect are by far the most common.

Cadential $^6_4$. Chord Ic, preceding chord V or V^7 in a perfect or imperfect cadence.

Canon. A strict form of imitation, often lasting for a substantial passage or entire piece, where the second part is an exact (or almost exact) copy of the first, even if at a different pitch.

Cantata. Most commonly a work for voice(s) and instruments in several movements, with aria(s), recitative(s) and chorus(es). A cantata can be sacred or secular.

Cantus firmus. An already-existing melody (frequently plainchant or a chorale) to which other freely-composed parts are added to make a new piece.

Chorale. A German hymn of the kind sung in the Lutheran (Protestant) church in the time of J. S. Bach. The word 'chorale' can refer to the words only, to the associated melody only, or to the whole hymn. Chorale melodies are largely stepwise (or conjunct); their harmonisation has long featured in advanced music courses.

Chordal. A form of homophony in which all the parts move together in the same or very similar rhythm (perhaps with very limited independent rhythmic movement). The term **homorhythmic** (literally 'same rhythm') is sometimes used instead.

Chromatic. A chromatic note is one that does not belong to the scale of the key currently in use. For example, in D major the notes G♯ and C♮ are chromatic. Music described as chromatic contains many chromatic notes.

Circle of 5ths. Harmonic progression in which the roots of the chords move by descending 5ths (and/or ascending 4ths), e.g. B–E–A–D–G–C etc.

Coda. A concluding section of a movement.

Concertato. Concertato style, used mainly in the first half of the 17th century, involved contrasts between different groups of performers, usually both vocal and instrumental.

Concerto. Most commonly, a work for a soloist with orchestra. In many concertos the solo instrument is a piano or a violin. Occasionally there may be two soloists (a double concerto) or even three (a triple concerto). (In the 17th century the term was used more widely, and was applied originally to a work in which voices and instruments, with more or less independent parts, collaborated in a manner that was new at the time.)

Conjunct. Melodic movement by step rather than by leap. Opposite of **disjunct**.

Continuo. Short for 'basso continuo' (Italian for 'continuous bass'), and used chiefly in Baroque music. Refers to an instrumental bass line (most commonly played by cello(s), sometimes with bass(es)), together with an improvised accompaniment on keyboard or lute, which supplies full harmony that might otherwise be lacking.

Contrapuntal. Adjective to describe music that uses **counterpoint**.

Contrary motion. Movement of two parts in opposite directions (e.g. soprano C–D–E, bass E–D–C).

Counterpoint. Counterpoint involves two or more melodic lines (usually rhythmically contrasted), each significant in itself, which are played or sung together.

Cross rhythm. The use of two or more very different rhythms simultaneously in different parts. One rhythm may imply one metre (or time signature), while another implies a different one.

Development. The central part of a sonata form movement between the exposition and the recapitulation, containing a working-out of ideas already heard in the exposition.

Dialogue. When two or more instruments or voices have a musical 'conversation', with the individual parts responding to one another.

Diatonic. Using notes that belong to the current key. A diatonic note is one that belongs to the scale of the key currently in use. For example, in D major the notes D, E and F♯ are diatonic.

Diminished-7th chord. A four-note chord made up of superimposed minor 3rds (or their **enharmonic equivalents**).

Diminished interval. An interval that is one semitone narrower than a minor or perfect interval. A diminished 4th (e.g. G♯–C) is one semitone narrower than a perfect 4th (G–C); a diminished 6th (e.g. B–G♭) is one semitone narrower than a minor 6th (B–G).

Diminution. The shortening of the rhythmic values of a previously-heard melody (e.g. where ♩♩♩ has become ♪♪♪).

Disjunct. Melodic movement by leap rather than by step. Opposite of **conjunct**.

Dissonance. Any note not a major or minor 3rd or 6th, perfect 5th, unison or perfect octave above the lowest part sounding is strictly a dissonance. Triads in root position or in first inversion are therefore the only chords that have no dissonance. (Even the 4th above the bass in a second inversion counts as dissonant.) Some dissonances, particularly suspensions and appoggiaturas, add harmonic tension and can help make the music more expressive; others, notably passing and auxiliary notes, provide rhythmic and melodic decoration. Although 'dissonance' and 'discord' are in some ways similar, dissonance is usually more to do with tension than with any deliberate roughness or harshness of sound that might be implied by the word discord.

Double-stopping. The playing of two notes simultaneously on adjacent strings of a string instrument. The term is sometimes used loosely to cover three- and four-note multiple stopping.

Échappée. An échappée (or 'escape note') leaves a harmony note by step (usually upwards) and then leaps in the opposite direction (usually by a 3rd) to a new harmony note.

Enharmonic (enharmonic equivalents). The same pitch notated in two different ways, e.g. B♭ and A♯. This can also be applied to intervals: e.g. the minor 3rds C–E♭ and B♯–D♯ and the augmented 2nd C–D♯ are all enharmonically equivalent to one another.

Exposition. The first section of a sonata form movement, typically including the first subject in the tonic and the second subject in a related key.

Expressionism. One of the most important musical movements of the 20th century, led by the composers Arnold Schoenberg, Alban Berg and Anton Webern. As the name suggests, it applies to music in which a composer's inner turmoil is reflected in unsettled, chaotic music.

False relation. The occurrence of the ordinary and chromatically altered versions of the same note (such as F♮ and F♯) in two different parts at the same time, or in close proximity.

Figured bass. A figured bass is an instrumental bass part with 'figures' or 'figuring' (chiefly numerals and sharp, flat and natural signs) designed to show a continuo keyboard or lute player what type of chord to play.

Fugue. A type of piece in which a theme called a 'subject' is treated in imitation by all the parts (usually with short passages called 'episodes' from which it is absent, for relief and contrast).

Functional harmony. A type of harmony that has the function of defining a major or minor key, most of all through chords on the tonic and dominant (I and V), with special emphasis on **perfect cadences**.

Galliard. A fast triple-time dance of the Renaissance era, usually consisting of three repeated sections (A A, B B, C C). It was frequently paired with a pavane.

Glissando. A slide between two notes.

Gigue. A piece whose ancestor is the jig, a dance of British origin. In a suite it normally comes at the end. Quick and lively, and generally in $\frac{12}{8}$ or other compound time.

Harmony note. A note that belongs to the chord being played or sung. For example, an F♯ in the melody is a harmony note in a chord of D major, whereas a G would be a non-harmony note.

Hemiola. The articulation of two units of triple time (strong-weak-weak, strong-weak-weak) as three units of duple time (strong-weak, strong-weak, strong-weak).

Heterophonic. In a heterophonic texture, a melody is performed simultaneously with one or more rhythmically and/or melodically varied versions of itself.

Homophonic. In a homophonic texture, one part has a melody and the other parts accompany, in contrast to contrapuntal writing, where each part has independent melodic and rhythmic interest.

Homorhythmic. *See* **Chordal**.

Hymn. A strophic vocal piece based on a metrical text, usually associated with services of the Christian church, commonly for congregation, with or without choir.

Imitation. Where a melodic idea in one part is immediately repeated in another part (exactly or inexactly), at the same or a different pitch, while the first part continues.

Imperfect cadence. An open-ended or inconclusive cadence ending with the dominant chord (V). The preceding chord is usually I, ii or IV.

Impressionism. A compositional movement that began in France in the late 19th century and continued into the 20th, and was in some respects similar to the art movement of the same name. Important characteristics of impressionist music include heightened attention to timbre, colour and atmosphere, non-functional harmony and tonality and fluid metre.

Interrupted cadence. A cadence intended to create surprise or suspense, perhaps by delaying the arrival of a final perfect or plagal cadence. Usually an interrupted cadence consists of chord V followed by chord VI.

Inversion. When a chord has a note other than the root in the lowest part, it is an inversion. In a first-inversion chord the 3rd of the chord is in the lowest part, and in a second-inversion chord the 5th. For example, a triad of F major in first inversion is A–C–F, and in second inversion is C–F–A. *See also* **Root position**.

Klangfarbenmelodie. German for 'sound-colour-melody'. A 20th-century musical technique associated particularly with composers such as Schoenberg and Webern, in which a melodic line is distributed among two or more different instruments, rather than played throughout by the same instrument, to provide heightened interest in terms of timbre and colour.

Leading note. The seventh degree of a major or minor scale, usually with a strong tendency to rise to the tonic.

Madrigal. Madrigals are normally secular (non-church) songs, often about love in a country setting. Most are for unaccompanied voices, but some from Monteverdi's time have basso continuo and perhaps other instruments.

March. A piece with a strong regular rhythm, generally in simple quadruple or duple metre, suitable for the military to march to; however, the march has also become a type of art music which is particularly useful in evoking patriotic or warlike situations.

Melismatic. The setting of several notes to one syllable.

Middle eight. In popular music, a contrasting section, often lasting eight bars, that prepares for the return of the main section.

Miniature. A short instrumental piece that depicts a scene or represents a mood.

Minimalist. Minimalist music emerged in the 1960s and 1970s in opposition to the increasingly remote and obscure modernist tendencies of such composers as Boulez and Stockhausen. Unlike modernist music, it is tonal or modal, continuous and often deliberately simple with much repetition of melodic and rhythmic patterns.

Minuet. A dance in simple triple metre of French origin. 17th- and 18th-century composers often included pieces entitled 'Minuet' in suites and symphonies, but for listening to, not for dancing. A minuet was generally played through twice, with a 'trio' in between (another minuet in all but name). Most minuets were graceful and not very fast.

Modal. A term often used to refer to music based on a mode rather than on major and minor keys. *See also* **Aeolian mode**.

Modulation. A change of key, or the process of changing key.

Monophonic. Consisting only of a single melodic line.

Motet. A type of church music for choir, sometimes accompanied by organ, and occasionally by larger forces. A motet often has Latin words (commonly from the Bible), and is particularly but not exclusively associated with Roman Catholic services.

Motif. A short but distinctive musical idea that is developed in various ways in order to create a longer passage of music.

Neapolitan 6th chord. A chromatic chord (often in a minor key) consisting of the first inversion of the major chord formed on the flattened supertonic, i.e. the flattened second degree of the scale (in D minor, for example, the Neapolitan sixth has the notes G–B♭–E♭).

Neoclassical. In music the adjective 'neoclassical' is most widely applied to certain early and mid 20th-century styles that combine a clear debt to previous eras (notably the Baroque and the Classical) with more up-to-date elements.

Octatonic scale. A scale with *eight* different notes (rather than the seven of a major or minor scale). In particular, a scale in which the intervals between notes are alternately tones and semitones.

Opera. A large-scale dramatic work for singers and instrumentalists. In most cases the whole text is sung, so that an opera is very different from a play with incidental music. An opera differs from a musical, too (for example, the music is not generally popular in idiom).

Ornamentation. Addition of melodic decoration, often through the use of conventional forms such as trills and mordents.

Ostinato. A repeating melodic, harmonic or rhythmic motif, heard continuously throughout part or the whole of a piece.

Outro. A section that finishes off a piece of music; its name is derived from 'intro', short for 'introduction'.

Parallel motion. Movement of two or more parts in the same direction, with the interval between them remaining essentially the same. Parallel 3rds (usually with a mixture of major and minor 3rds) are common in many styles; parallel perfect 5ths are avoided in some.

Passing note. A non-harmony note approached and quitted by step in the same direction, often filling in a melodic gap of a 3rd (e.g. A between G and B, where both G and B are harmony notes).

Pavane. Slow, quadruple-time dance of the Renaissance era, usually consisting of three repeated sections (A A, B B, C C).

Pedal note. A sustained or repeated note, usually in a low register, over which changing harmonies occur. A pedal on the fifth note of the scale (a 'dominant pedal') tends to create a sense of expectation in advance of a perfect cadence; a pedal on the keynote (a 'tonic pedal') can create a feeling of repose.

Pentatonic. A scale made up of five notes, most frequently the first, second, third, fifth and sixth degrees of a major scale (for example, C pentatonic is C–D–E–G–A).

Perfect cadence. A cadence ending with the tonic chord (I), preceded by the dominant (V or V⁷) – appropriate where some degree of finality is required.

Phrygian cadence. A type of imperfect cadence, in which the dominant chord (V) is preceded by the first inversion of the subdominant (IVb). It is used chiefly in minor keys, and particularly in Baroque music.

Pizzicato (often abbreviated to **pizz.**). A direction to pluck, instead of bow, string(s) on a violin, viola, cello or double bass. Cancelled by the direction 'arco' – with the bow.

Plagal cadence. A cadence ending with the tonic chord (I), preceded by the subdominant (IV). Appropriate where a restful finality is required, it is used sparingly in tonal music.

Pointillism. The term 'pointillism' originally referred to a painting technique, in which (rather than depict an object realistically) small dots of colour were carefully placed to give the impression of that object when viewed from a distance. In music, particularly some serial music of the mid 20th century, the composer employed isolated sounds and tiny groups of sounds in a way that invites comparison with pointillism in art. *See also* **Klangfarbenmelodie**.

Polyphonic. The term 'polyphonic' has a similar meaning to **contrapuntal**, but tends to be used for vocal, not instrumental music. In Medieval and Renaissance music, use of the adjective 'polyphonic' can imply a distinction between music in several voice-parts and monophonic plainsong.

Polyrhythm. Two or more distinct rhythms, not commonly divisible (for example a triplet and a quintuplet), played at the same time.

Portamento. A slide between two notes. The term is applied more usually in vocal music.

Post-modern. Modernism in the arts stressed tension, change and originality and often a highly intellectual approach (as in serialism) until the 1960s and 70s. After – 'post' – this modernist tendency, some composers, have developed new styles of 'classical' music which are less demanding emotionally and intellectually, and which have somewhat broader appeal.

Prima prattica. Term applied, originally by theorists in the early Baroque period, to music of the Renaissance era.

Push. A form of syncopation in pop music, in which a note that falls on a strong beat is anticipated and sounded early.

Recapitulation. In **sonata form**, the section which follows the development. It is often closely based on the exposition, but normally both opens and closes in the tonic key.

Reggae. A genre of popular music originating in Jamaica, with roots in ska and rocksteady. It has a distinctive rhythmic style characterised by off-beat accents.

Relative major and minor. Keys that have the same key signature but a different scale (e.g. F major and D minor, both with a key signature of one flat). A relative minor is three semitones lower than its relative major (e.g. the tonic of D minor is three semitones lower than the tonic of its relative major, F major).

Retrograde. The pitches of a previously heard melody or rhythm presented in reverse order.

Rhythm and blues. A harder-edged form of blues which emerged in American cities in the 1940s.

Riff. A short, catchy melodic figure, repeated like an **ostinato** and commonly found in rock, pop and jazz.

Ritornello form. A structure used in Baroque music in which an opening instrumental section (called the **ritornello**) introduces the main musical ideas. This returns, often in shortened versions and in related keys, between passages for one or more soloists. The complete ritornello (or a substantial part of it) returns in the tonic key at the end.

Rockabilly. An early form of rock 'n' roll, which takes its name from 'rock' and 'hillbilly' (a term for inhabitants of rural regions of the USA, referring to the country music that influenced rockabilly). It developed in the 1950s before waning in popularity in the 1960s, but was later revived in the late 1970s.

Rocksteady. An early form of reggae, emerging in the late 1960s.

Rondo. A piece in which an opening section in the tonic key is heard several times, with different material ('episodes'), usually in different keys, between these repetitions. The simplest rondo shape is A B A C A (where A is the recurring section and B and C are episodes), but this can be extended, for instance with additional episode(s) and further repeats of the A section.

Root position. A chord which has the root in the lowest sounding part.

Saltarello. A lively folk dance in $\frac{6}{8}$ originating in southern Italy.

Sarabande. In its most common form during the Baroque period, a slow dance in $\frac{3}{4}$, often with an emphasis on the second beat.

Seconda prattica. Term applied, originally by contemporary theorists, to music of the early Baroque era to distinguish it from that of the preceding Renaissance style.

Sequence. Immediate repetition of a melodic or harmonic idea at a different pitch.

Serial. In serial music all (or most) pitches are derived from an underlying fixed series of pitches which can be manipulated by transposition, inversion and retrograding (being played backwards). A widely practised form of serialism in the mid 20th century used a series (or 'row') of twelve notes that included every note of the chromatic scale once.

Sextuplet. A group of six equal notes played in the time normally taken by four notes of the same type.

Sonata. An instrumental work, commonly in three or four movements. From the late Baroque period onwards, sonatas are usually for solo keyboard or for single melody instrument and keyboard. 'Trio sonatas' (middle to late Baroque) are normally for two violins and continuo.

Sonata form. A form developed in the Classical period from binary form. The first section is the exposition, beginning in the tonic and ending in a closely-related key, often with two contrasting groups of melodic material (first subject, second subject). The second section commonly includes a development section, followed by a recapitulation with first and second subjects restated in the tonic.

Strophic. A strophic song is one in which each stanza has the same (or very similar) music.

Suspension. A suspension occurs at a change of chord, when one part hangs on to (or repeats) a note from the old chord, creating a clash, after which the delayed part resolves by step (usually down) to a note of the new chord.

Swung rhythm. In jazz and other popular music, a certain freedom in performance whereby rhythms that might in other contexts be played 'straight' (as equal notes) are performed with the first of each pair longer than the second, often with a kind of triplet effect.

Syllabic. The setting of one note to one syllable.

Symphonic poem. A type of programme music for orchestra, depicting a character, mood or idea or telling a story. Also known as a **tone poem**.

Symphony. A work for orchestra with several (usually three or four) movements in different tempi – in effect a **sonata** for orchestra rather than for one or a few instruments.

Syncopation. The shifting of stress from a strong to a weak beat. For example, in a $\frac{4}{4}$ bar with the rhythm ♩ ♩ ♩, the minim (a relatively long note beginning on a weak beat) is syncopated.

Ternary form. A musical structure of three sections in which the outer sections are similar and the central one contrasting (ABA).

Texture. The relationship between the various simultaneous lines in a passage of music, dependent on such features as the number and function of the parts and the spacing between them.

Theme and variations. A instrumental compositional form in which an initial melodic or harmonic theme is heard, and then developed by the composer. Often, the theme is repeated at the end of the piece, to give a sense of closure.

Through-composed. A song that uses mainly different music for each verse of the text.

Tierce de Picardie. A major 3rd in the final tonic chord of a passage in a minor key.

Transition. A linking passage. *See* **Bridge passage**.

Tremolo. A rapid and continuous repetition of a single note or two alternating notes.

Trill. An ornament in which two adjacent notes rapidly and repeatedly alternate (the note bearing the trill sign and the one above it). The symbol for a trill is *tr*.

Tripartite. Meaning 'having three parts', this refers to works in three distinct sections.

Triple-stopping. The playing of three notes simultaneously (or as near simultaneously as possible) on adjacent strings of a string instrument.

Triplet. A group of three equal notes played in the time normally taken by two notes of the same type. For example, a triplet of quavers is played in the time taken by two normal quavers.

Tritone. *See* **Augmented 4th**.

Turnaround. In jazz and pop, a short link leading to the next section.

Twelve-bar blues. A standard chord sequence lasting 12 bars, used in the blues and other popular music. It is based on the tonic (I), subdominant (IV) and dominant (V) chords of a key. A common form is I–I–I–I, IV–IV–I–I, V–IV–I–I.

Unison. Simultaneous performance of the same note or melody by two or more players or singers.

Viol. A bowed, fretted string instrument common in the Renaissance and early Baroque periods. A consort of viols consists of instruments of different sizes and pitches, from soprano down to bass.

Vocalisation. A style of singing in which pitches are produced without distinct words. The term often refers to technical exercises for singers which focus on vowels, but composers have written textless vocal pieces for performance.

Whole-tone scale. A scale in which the interval between every successive note is a whole tone.

Copyright